Letterhead 5

An International Collection of Letterhead Design
Briefpapiergestaltung im internationalen Überblick
Une compilation internationale sur le design de papiers à lettres

CEO & Creative Director: B. Martin Pedersen

Publisher: Doug Wolske
Publications Director: Michael Gerbino

Editors: Andrea Birnbaum and Heinke Jenssen

Art Director: Lauren Slutsky
Design & Production Assistant: Joseph Liotta

Published by Graphis Inc.

(opposite: Templin Brink Design for KEA)

Contents InhaltSommaire

Remarks: We extend our heartfelt thanks to contributors throughout the world who have made it possible to publish a wide and international spectrum of the best work in this field. Entry instructions for all Graphis Books may be requested from: **Graphis Inc.**, 307 Fifth Avenue, Tenth Floor, New York, NY 10016, or visit our Web site at www.graphis.com. Anmerkungen: Unser Dank gilt den Einsendern aus aller Welt, die es uns ermöglicht haben, ein breites, internationales Spektrum der besten Arbeiten zu veröffentlichen. Teilnahmebe-din-gungen für die Graphis-Bücher sind erhältlich bei: **Graphis Inc.**, 307 Fifth Avenue, Tenth Floor, New York, USA. Besuchen Sie uns im World Wide Web, www.graphis.com. Remerciements: Nous remercions les participants du monde entier qui ont rendu possible la publication de cet ouvrage offrant un panorama complet des meilleurs travaux. Les modalités d'inscription peuvent être obtenues auprès de: **Graphis Inc.**, 307 Fifth Avenue, Tenth Floor, New York, NY 10016. Rendez-nous visite sur notre site web: www.graphis.com. © Copyright under universal copyright convention copyright © 2001 by Graphis Inc., 307 Fifth Avenue, Tenth Floor, New York, NY 10016. Jacket and book design copyright © 2001 by Graphis, Inc. No part of this book may be reproduced in any form without written permission of the publisher. ISBN: 1-888001-73-9 Printed in Hong Kong.

(opposite: Studio d Design for Belkowitz Photography & Film)

Variety and Surprise by Gerard Hadders

In the late 1980s, I had a conversation with a design manager of a major insurance company about the future of printed house-style items. At the time, IT developments were soaring, and within 3 years, all major companies would be using only out-of-printer letterheads. Maybe this guy was the last modernist (and *not* Samuel Beckett), but in a sense he stood blind to the typical phenomena that would typify the 90s; Information Technology (IT) turned into Information and Communication Technology (ICT), and youthful individualism became the most sought after identity claim. In other words: stronger unification as a typical 80s technology promise became obsolete with the development of new management strategies and the internet, which thrive on variety and surprise. Gimmicky house-style items were abundant in the early 90s. Exuberant form, color, typography and finishing as celebration of individualism design seemed to be defined by esthetics. This exuberance of form was replaced by exuberance of (*ahem*) content. Or was it? Tibor Kalman's moral rationalism and David Carson's neo-surrealism ruled for a while, until it all became replaced by internet buttons and flags, or as I call them: pills (>illustr 1). The designed item no longer related to print culture but to a new media that was becoming mainstream. It took on, interestingly enough, a style that developed from the limitations of web design. Of course, one of the main events was the rise of what used to be called the media director—the graphic design version of the advertising art director, who moves as easily between print and cyberspace as the classical fine artist did between bronze and oils. Young people pouring into graphic design no longer had the ambition to fiddle endlessly around to get the right mood at the right place on 48cm2 or less. They no longer punched holes in paper but in time.

New Helvetica, New Futura, New Univers. By the looks of many graphic designs, we're back in the 60s again. But where the grids of the functionalists served to structure a text by content, like say: a fishing net, today's young and brave go for the esthetic value of the grid, like say: a Sol LeWitt structural sculpture. It could also be a computer screen induced deterioration of eyesight that creates a strong craving for the simple form, and then over and over again. And then when, a couple of years ago, designers couldn't find the round corner filter anymore, we became stuck with square pills (>illustr 2).

Neopostretrofunctionalism. Or was it Neoretropostfunctionalism? Is style dead again? Does style matter? A designer has to accept the fact that in a competitive communication culture, style is the message. To get stuck with one style is professional suicide. Graphic designers tend to grow professionally as the result of a chain of commissions. These commissions usually generate one central form or method of expression in a designer. With industrial design or architecture, where models play an important role, new standards have been created through designs that were never even executed. Simply because of a tradition of publishing prototypes and models,

these other applied arts can develop without the benefits of a client culture. So: *ahem*, content again. Designers have to develop an equivalent to the architecture model, where the entire process is built into a simulation that represents the real thing, structure and all, not just the surface. Young designers need to concentrate more on process and development, on preconditions that matter for the client and the product. Most students have mainly been trained in esthetics, or line and color. I find confronting them with content is much like bringing back the dead.

The new/old freshness of the Arts and Crafts movement brought civil society a means to express itself individually, esthetically and, maybe, a bit mediaevally. And it is, at least in the Netherlands, where the history of 'modern design' begins. That is why I find it very interesting that a recent product by the Dutch type design duo of Just van Rossem en Erik van Blokland, Letterror, is a toolkit based on the dollar-bill typeface. Very Old School indeed! Letterror work like the English writers, engravers and publishers (all in one) of the 'Glorious Revolution.' They write, design, code and distribute. Their way of thinking follows through from model to product. And in doing so they constantly question the conditions of contemporary graphic communication. As such, they come as close to a tasking formula as is necessary in graphic design.

One of Letterror's early inventions was a typeface that would be unpredictable in its printed form (>Illustr 3). Just imagine that printer embedded typefaces like truetype would be replaced by a number of unpredictable typefaces like the Kosmik. Or that a similar function would be built into printer software. Then it would be highly interesting again to develop out of printer letterheads, as was once a prophecy of my old design manager friend. Is it possible that variety and surprise replace predictability as a corporate communication tool? Just imagine a database that adds the ages of clients to its mailing list (>illustr 4). This would be a better personalization than a printed signature.

Computerized communication in its advent had a tendency to expel the individual. The effort, cost and limitations of automated systems couldn't handle it. The early Mac revolution didn't really improve on this situation. Because of the great demolition race the graphic industry went through in the same period, designers were forced to absorb responsibilities that used to belong to typesetters and lithographers. By now, the industry has resettled and things are looking up again. The new generation of personal computers is so powerful that the individual can truly compete with high-end systems. But it's each designer's choice to use this new acquired freedom to create an efficient cottage industry or to challenge the big boys and their game.

Gerard Hadders, born in 1954 in Rotterdam, is a fine artist, designer, photographer and tutor of the Postgraduate Graphic Design Course at St.Joost Academy in Holland. He co-founded Hard Werken Magazine and the firm of Hard Werken Design, as well as Qwerty Magazine. Hadders is the winner of such prestigious awards as the Werkman Prize of the city of Amsterdam, for his Graphic Oeuvre, and of the Kodak Best Photo Book Award. He has lectured and exhibited extensively throughout Europe. Since 1993, he has run his own company, Buro Lange Haven, in the Netherlands. Hadders is also founder and partner of Del*Uxe, research + design, and of S.T.I.P. (System Typography Integrated Program).

Vielfältiges und Überraschendes von Gerard Hadders

Ich erinnere mich an ein Gespräch, das ich Ende der achtziger Jahre mit einem Design-Manager einer grossen Versicherungsgesellschaft hatte. Es ging dabei um die technologische Entwicklung und die Zukunft von Briefschaften. Seiner Meinung nach würden alle grossen Firmen innerhalb der nächsten drei Jahre nur noch mit dem Computer ausgedrucktes Briefpapier verwenden. Vielleicht war er der letzte Modernist (und nicht Samuel Beckett), aber ein Phänomen, das die frühen neunziger Jahre kennzeichnen sollte, hatte er nicht vorausgesehen: Aus IT (Information Technology) wurde ICT (Information and Communication Technology), und jugendlicher Individualismus prägte das visuelle Erscheinungsbild der

meisten Firmen. Das heisst, obwohl aufgrund der neuen Technologie in den achtziger Jahren vor allem eine stärkere Vereinheitlichung prognostiziert wurde, geschah das Gegenteil: Neue Management-Strategien und das Internet führten stattdessen zu sehr unterschiedlichen und überraschenden Lösungen.

Wo man auch hinsah, in den frühen neunziger Jahren ging es bei den Firmenauftritten um Effekthascherei. Individualismus war angesagt, und es schien allein um die optische Wirkung zu gehen: Formen, Farben, Typographie und spezielle Effekte dominierten. Auf diesen überschwenglichen Gebrauch von Form folgte ein überschwenglicher

Gebrauch von Inhalt. Oder nicht? Eine Zeit lang dominierten Tibor Kalmans moralischer Rationalismus und David Carsons Neo-Surrealismus, bevor alles etwas anderem wich - den Schaltflächen des Internets, oder, wie ich sie nenne, den "Pillen" (Pills) . Die Gestaltung eines Firmenauftritts hatte nichts mehr mit der Kunst und der Kultur des Druckens zu tun, sondern mit einem neuen Medium, das zum Allgemeingut wurde. Es entwickelte sich interessanterweise ein Stil, der seinen Ursprung in den Beschränkungen des Web-Designs hatte. Im Zuge dieser Entwicklung tauchte auch der Media Director auf, wie man ihn seinerzeit nannte. Darunter ist die Graphik-Design-Version dessen zu verstehen, was der Art Director in einer Werbeagentur ist, jemand, der sich mühelos zwischen Druckmedien, CD-ROM und Internet bewegt. Ähnlich wie ein klassischer Künstler Malerei und Plastik, musste er sämtliche Medien beherrschen. Der Nachwuchs der Graphic-Design-Branche mühte sich nicht mehr endlos damit ab, die richtige Stimmung am richtigen Platz auf einem höchstens 48 cm2 grossen Papier hinzubekommen. Es ging nicht mehr ums Papier, sondern um Zeit.

Neue Helvetica, Neue Futura, Neue Univers – wenn nicht alles täuscht, sind wir unterdes wieder in den sechziger Jahren angelangt. Aber während die Seitenraster der Funktionalisten dazu dienten, einen Text dem Inhalt entsprechend zu strukturieren, ihn quasi wie in einem Fischernetz aufzunehmen, geht es den mutigen jungen Designern von heute um die ästhetische Qualität des Rasters, vergleichbar mit Sol LeWitts Kombinationen geometrischer Elemente. Es wäre auch möglich, dass die

eine Simulation des Arbeitsprozesses, die den realen Gegenstand, den Aufbau und all das berücksichtigt, statt sich nur auf die Oberfläche zu beschränken. Die jungen Designer müssen sich auf Aufbau und Entwicklung konzentrieren, auf die Voraussetzungen, die für den Kunden und das Produkt wichtig sind.

Die Arts-and-Crafts-Bewegung gab seinerzeit der Gesellschaft die Möglichkeit, sich individuell, ästhetisch und - vielleicht - ein bisschen altmodisch auszudrücken. Hiermit begann, zumindest in den Niederlanden, die Geschichte des modernen Designs. In diesem Zusammenhang finde ich es höchst interessant, dass ein kürzlich lanciertes Produkt von Letterror, dem holländischen Typographie-Designer-Duo Just van Rossem und Erik van Blokland, auf der Schrift der Dollar-Note basiert. Das ist in der Tat sehr alte Schule. Letterror arbeitet ähnlich wie die englischen Schriftsteller der "Glorreichen Revolution", die gleichzeitig Autoren, Graveure und Verleger waren; die Partner schreiben, entwerfen Schriften, schreiben Programme und vertreiben ihre Produkte. Ihr Denkprozess beginnt beim Modellentwurf und endet beim Produkt, und sie stellen die heutige graphische Kommunikation immer wieder in Frage. Sie haben einen Arbeitsprozess entwickelt, wie er im Graphic Design erforderlich ist.

Eine der frühen Erfindungen von Letterror war eine Schrift, deren gedruckte Form sich nicht voraussagen liess. Man stelle sich vor, dass im Drucker installierte "Truetype"-Schriften von einer Anzahl in ihrem Ausdruck nicht vorhersehbarer Schriften wie "Kosmik" ersetzt werden würden. Oder eine ähnliche Funktion würde in die Drucker-Software

1   2   3   4

durch den Bildschirm verursachte Beeinträchtigung der Sehkraft zu einem starken Verlangen nach einfachen Formen geführt hat, und in der Folge nach immer einfacheren. Und schliesslich konnten die Designer vor ein paar Jahren den Filter für die runden Formen nicht mehr finden - deshalb haben wir nun nichts als eckige Schaltflächen.

Erleben wir einen Neopostretrofunktionalismus oder vielleicht doch eher einen Neoretropostfunktionalismus? Ist Stil wieder einmal tot? Ist Stil wichtig? Ein Designer muss sich damit abfinden, dass in einer vom Wettbewerb bestimmten Kommunikationskultur Stil die Botschaft ist. Sich auf einen bestimmten Stil zu beschränken, ist beruflicher Selbstmord. Normalerweise sammelt ein Graphic Designer seine Erfahrungen durch eine Reihe von Aufträgen, und diese führen im allgemeinen dazu, dass er eine bestimmte Methode oder Ausdrucksform entwickelt. Im Industriedesign oder in der Architektur, wo Modelle eine wichtige Rolle spielen, wurden durch Entwürfe, auch wenn sie nie realisiert wurden, neue Massstäbe geschaffen. Dank dieser Tradition, mit Prototypen oder Modellen zu arbeiten, findet im Industriedesign und in der Architektur auch ohne die Einflüsse von Auftraggebern eine Entwicklung statt. Ich habe festgestellt, dass ich Tote zum Leben erwecken muss, wenn ich vor Graphic Design Studenten über Inhalte spreche, die meisten haben nur etwas über Ästhetik gelernt, über Linien und Farben. Durch die neuen Werkzeuge wird Graphik-Design immer komplizierter. Die Designer müssen sich etwas schaffen, das dem Modell der Architekten entspricht –

eingebaut werden. Dann wäre es in der Tat wieder sehr interessant, mit vom Drucker ausgedrucktem Briefpapier zu arbeiten, so wie mein alter Freund, der Design-Manager, es vorausgesagt hatte. Ist es möglich, dass Vielfalt und Überraschung statt Vorhersehbarkeit zum Instrument der Firmenkommunikation werden? Man stelle sich das vor: Die Firmen würden das Alter ihrer Kunden in ihren Dateien speichern und ihren graphischen Auftritt entsprechend anpassen. Das würde zu einer weitaus persönlicheren Ansprache führen als Korrespondenz mit einer gedruckten Unterschrift.

Die Kommunikation per Computer hatte zunächst zur Folge, dass eine individuelle Ansprache fast unmöglich wurde. Der Aufwand, die Kosten und die Beschränkungen dieses automatisierten Systems liessen es einfach nicht zu. Auch die Mac-Revolution konnte an dieser Situation nicht wirklich etwas ändern. Die Auswirkungen der neuen Technologie bedeuteten für Teile der graphischen Industrie das Ende, während die Graphic Designer andererseits die Arbeit von Setzern und Lithographen übernehmen mussten. Inzwischen ist eine gewisse Beruhigung in der Branche eingetreten, und vieles ist einfacher geworden. Die neue Generation von PCs ist so leistungsstark, dass sie – und damit der Benutzer - es ohne weiteres mit den Grossrechnern aufnehmen kann. Dabei bleibt es jedem Designer überlassen, ob er seine neu erworbene Freiheit dazu nutzt, sich zu spezialisieren oder sich am Spiel der Grossen zu beteiligen.

*Gerard Hadders, 1954 in Rotterdam geboren, ist Künstler, Designer, Photograph und Lehrer des Nachdiplomkurses für Graphic Design an der Akademie St. Joost in Breda, Niederlande. Er ist Mitbegründer der Firma Hard Werken Design und des gleichnamigen Magazins sowie des Qwerty Magazine. Er wurde u.a. mit dem hoch angesehenen Werkman-Preis der Stadt Amsterdam für seine graphisches Lebenswerk und mit dem Kodak-Preis für das schönste Photobuch ausgezeichnet. In ganz Europa ist er durch zahlreiche Ausstellungen und Vorträge bekannt. Seit 1993 führt er seine eigene Firma Buro Lange Haven in den Niederlanden. Ausserdem ist er Mitbegründer von Del*Uxe Research and Design sowie von S.T.I.P. (System Typography Integrated Program).*

*Né en 1954 à Rotterdam, Gerard Hadders est artiste, graphiste, photographe et professeur d'arts graphiques à l'Académie St. Joost, Breda, Pays-Bas. Il est cofondateur du magazines Hard Werken et Qwerty ainsi que de la société Hard Werken Design. Gerard Hadders a remporté des prix prestigieux, tels que le Werkman Prize de la cité d'Amsterdam pour son œuvre graphique et le Kodak Best Photo Book Award. Il a fréquemment exposé ses travaux en Europe et y a également donné de nombreuses conférences. Depuis 1993, il dirige sa propre société Buro Lange Haven aux Pays-Bas. Il est aussi cofondateur de Del*Uxe Research and Design et de S.T.I.P. (System Typography Integrated Program).*

Je me souviens d'une conversation que j'ai eue à la fin des années 80 avec le responsable de la division graphique d'une importante compagnie d'assurances. Notre discussion portait sur les technologies de l'information et leur influence sur les supports de correspondance des sociétés. Selon lui, toutes les grandes entreprises utiliseraient uniquement du papier à lettres imprimé à l'aide de l'ordinateur dans les trois prochaines années. Peut-être était-il le dernier moderniste (en lieu et place de Samuel Beckett). Toujours est-il qu'il n'avait pas prévu une évolution qui allait marquer les années 90: les technologies de l'information s'étaient transformées en technologies de l'information et de la communication, et les identités visuelles de la plupart des sociétés se caractérisaient par leur individualisme. Contrairement à ce que laissait supposer l'essor technologique des années 80, on n'assista pas à un phénomène d'uniformisation. Au contraire, les nouvelles stratégies de management et Internet furent à l'origine de solutions aussi surprenantes que variées.

Au début des années 90, les identités institutionnelles se devaient surtout de présenter une astuce, un truc pour attirer l'attention, l'individualisme était de mise et l'effet optique primait sur toute chose: une grande importance était accordée aux formes, souvent exubérantes, aux couleurs, à la typographie et à la finition. A cette abondance de formes succéda une abondance de contenu. Ou n'était-ce pas le cas? Pendant un certain temps, le rationalisme moral de Tibor Kalman et le néosurréalisme de David Carson s'imposèrent, avant que les boutons et drapeaux d'Internet, que j'appelle les "pilules", ne prennent le pas sur le reste. Une identité visuelle n'avait plus rien à voir avec une impression traditionnelle et soignée, mais avec un nouveau média bientôt adopté par tous. Fait intéressant, un style se développa, imposé par les contraintes du webdesign. Suite à cette évolution, un nouveau corps de métier vit le jour: le directeur média, comme on le désignait à l'époque. Il incarnait en quelque sorte la "version design graphique" du directeur artistique d'une agence de publicité, se sentant aussi à l'aise avec les médias imprimés, le CD-ROM et Internet qu'un artiste classique avec ses bronzes et ses huiles. Il devait maîtriser tous les médias. Les nouveaux venus dans la branche du design graphique ne passaient plus des heures entières à créer péniblement la bonne atmosphère sur le bon support, une feuille de papier de 48 cm2 au maximum. Ce n'était plus une question de papier, mais de temps.

Nouvelle Helvetica, nouvelle Futura, nouvelle Univers – au regard du design graphique actuel, j'ai l'impression, si je ne m'abuse, que nous avons fait un retour en arrière dans les années 60. Mais tandis que les trames des fonctionnalistes servaient à structurer un texte en fonction de son contenu, à le saisir en quelque sorte dans un filet de pêche, les jeunes designers se préoccupent actuellement davantage de la qualité esthétique de la trame, à l'image des combinaisons d'éléments géométriques de Sol LeWitt. Il est aussi possible qu'une baisse de l'acuité visuelle, due aux heures passées devant un écran d'ordinateur, ait généré ce besoin de formes simples, devenues, conséquence logique, toujours plus simples. Enfin, comme les designers ne pouvaient plus, il y a quelques années, se servir du filtre utilisé pour arrondir les formes, nous nous retrouvons aujourd'hui avec des boutons carrés.

Sommes-nous passés au néopostrétrofonctionnalisme ou plutôt au néorétropostfonctionnalisme? Le style est-il de nouveau mort? Le style est-il important? Un designer doit accepter que, dans une culture de communication marquée par l'esprit de compétition, le style est le message. Se limiter à un certain style est un suicide professionnel. En général, ce n'est qu'en exécutant divers mandats qu'un designer graphique acquerra de l'expérience et développera, ce faisant, une méthode ou une forme d'expression. Dans les domaines du design industriel et de l'architecture, où les

modèles jouent un rôle important, de nouveaux jalons ont été posés sur la base d'esquisses, même si celles-ci n'ont jamais été matérialisées. Grâce à cette tradition qui veut que l'on travaille avec des prototypes et des modèles, les secteurs du design industriel et de l'architecture peuvent évoluer, même si au bout du compte, il n'y a pas de client. Je me suis aperçu que les étudiants en arts graphiques tombent des nues lorsque je leur parle de contenus, car la plupart d'entre eux ont uniquement appris quelque chose sur l'esthétique, les lignes et les couleurs. Les nouveaux outils à disposition des graphistes rendent la discipline de plus en plus compliquée. Ceux-ci devraient développer un modèle qui corresponde à celui des architectes – simuler un processus de travail qui tienne compte de l'objet réel et de sa structure, au lieu de se limiter simplement à la surface. Les jeunes designers graphiques doivent se concentrer davantage sur le processus et le développement, sur les conditions qui sont importantes pour le client et le produit.

En son temps, l'arts & crafts movement a donné la possibilité à la société de s'exprimer tant sur le plan individuel qu'esthétique et – peut-être aussi – de façon quelque peu surannée. C'est ainsi qu'a débuté, du moins aux Pays-Bas, l'histoire du design moderne. Dans ce contexte, je trouve extrêmement intéressant qu'un produit récemment lancé par Letterror – le duo de designers/typographes hollandais Just van Rossem et Erik van Blokland – s'inspire du billet vert. C'est le retour à la vieille école. Letterror travaille selon le même principe que les écrivains britanniques durant la révolution en Angleterre (1688-89), qui étaient à la fois auteurs, graveurs et éditeurs; les deux associés de Letterror écrivent, conçoivent des polices de caractères, des programmes et se chargent de commercialiser leurs produits. Ils appliquent leur mode de pensée du début à la fin, de la conception du modèle au produit final, tout en remettant en question la communication graphique actuelle. Ils ont mis au point un procédé de travail qui fait cruellement défaut à la branche du design graphique.

L'une des premières inventions de Letterror était une police de caractères dont on ignorait comment elle se présenterait une fois imprimée. Imaginez-vous que les polices de l'ordinateur, par exemple les truetypes, étaient remplacées par des polices imprévues, telles que la Kosmik. Ou qu'une fonction similaire était installée dans le logiciel d'impression. Dans ce contexte, il serait à nouveau très intéressant de concevoir du papier à lettres imprimé à l'aide de l'ordinateur, ainsi que l'avait prédit mon vieil ami responsable du design. Est-il possible que les instruments de communication des sociétés ne soient plus prévisibles, mais variés et surprenants? Supposons, par exemple, que les entreprises entrent l'âge de leurs clients dans une banque de données et adaptent la typographie en conséquence. Par rapport à une signature imprimée par exemple, cela permettrait d'avoir une correspondance beaucoup plus personnalisée.

Dans un premier temps, la tendance dans la communication informatisée était d'exclure toute formule personnelle, car ce système automatisé aurait représenté des frais, une surcharge de travail et des contraintes par trop importants. La révolution du Mac n'a pas non plus permis de remédier à cette situation. Les nouvelles technologies ont condamné des pans entiers de l'industrie graphique à disparaître, tandis que les designers graphiques durent reprendre certaines activités des compositeurs et lithographes. Depuis, la branche connaît une période d'accalmie et nombre de tâches sont devenues plus simples. Les ordinateurs de la nouvelle génération sont si performants qu'ils – et par conséquent, leurs utilisateurs – peuvent fort bien rivaliser avec des systèmes ultrasophistiqués. Il n'en demeure pas moins que chaque designer est libre de choisir s'il veut tirer profit de cette liberté nouvellement acquise pour se spécialiser et trouver une niche de marché ou s'il veut jouer dans la cour des grands.

Jeana Lautigar, CPA
SMALL BUSINESS SPECIALIST

2800 WEST 44TH STREET
MINNEAPOLIS, MN 55410
PHONE: 612 928.3871

Jeana Lautigar, CPA
SMALL BUSINESS SPECIALIST

2800 WEST 44TH STREET
MINNEAPOLIS, MN 55410
PHONE: 612 928.3871

Jeana Lautigar, CPA
SMALL BUSINESS SPECIALIST

2800 WEST 44TH STREET
MINNEAPOLIS, MN 55410

Design Firm: **Xeno Group Inc.** Art Director: **Victor Wang** Designer: **Edgar Pardo** Client: **Xeno Group Inc.**

Accounting, Advertising 12,13

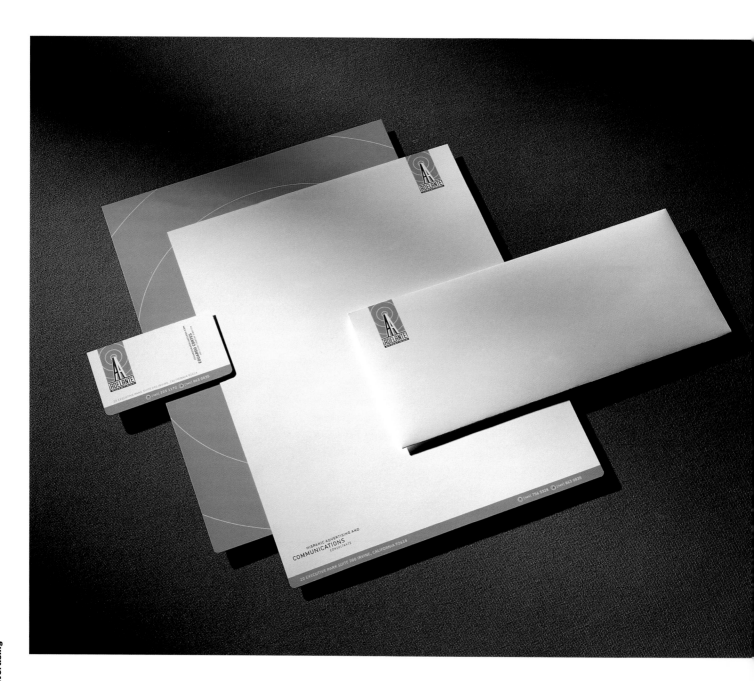

Craig Welsh

Welsh
P.O. Box 4103
Lancaster, PA 17601

717-285-4050 - T
717-285-7273 - F

cwelsh@gowelsh.com

Design Firm: **Welsh/DLD** Art Director: **Craig Welsh**

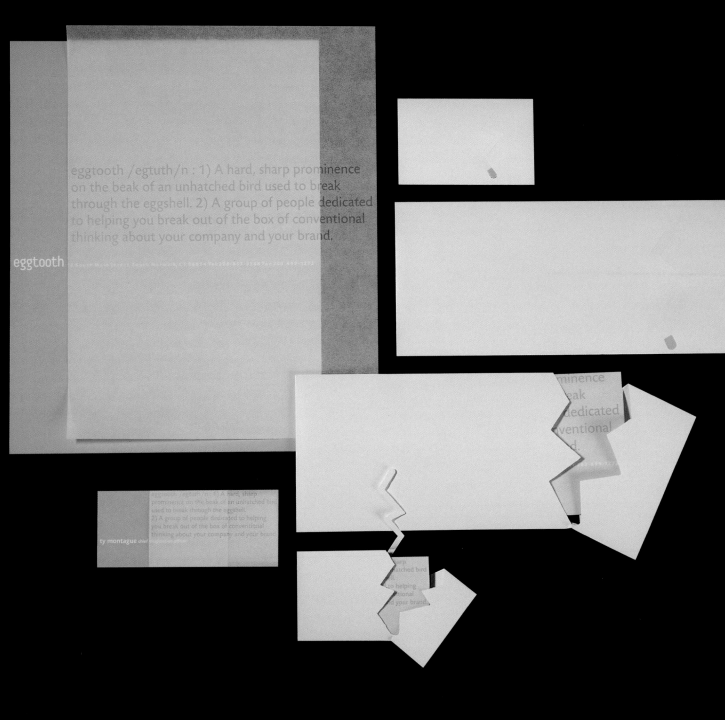

eggtooth /egtuth/n : 1) A hard, sharp prominence on the beak of an unhatched bird used to break through the eggshell. 2) A group of people dedicated to helping you break out of the box of conventional thinking about your company and your brand.

eggtooth

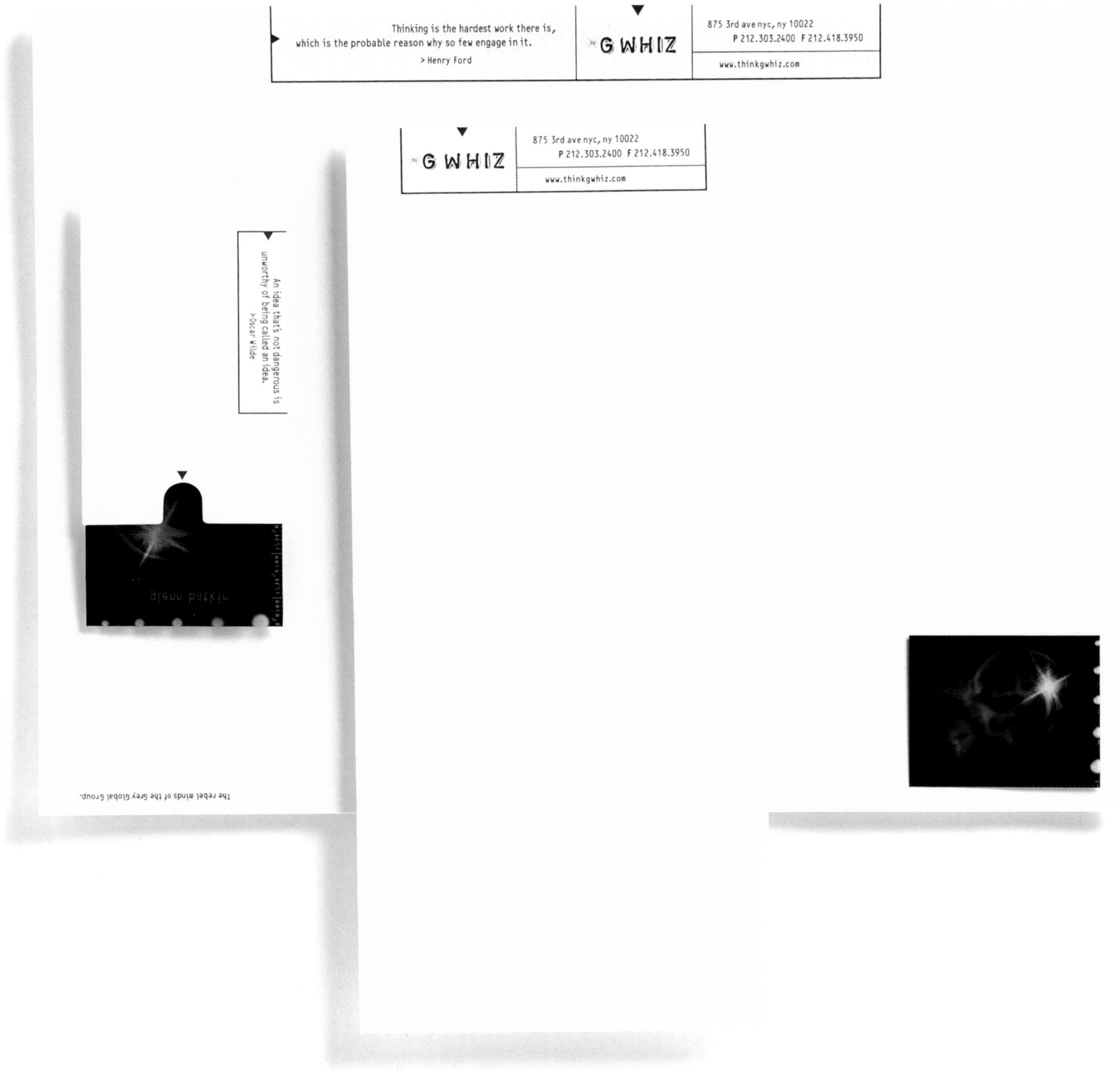

Design Firm: **GWHIZ** Art Director: **Glenn Batkin** Creative Directors: **Glenn Batkin** and **Brett Howlett** Designer: **Dasi Williams** Illustrator: **Atmosphere 13**

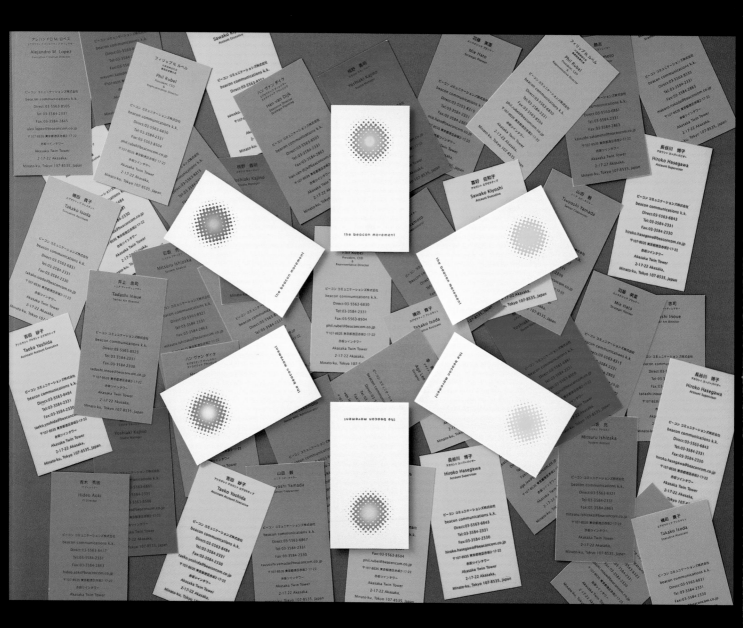

(this spread) Design Firm: **beacon communications kk** Art Director: **Mayumi Kato** Creative Director: **Alejandro M. Lopez** Designers: **Chie Arakawa, Misako Maruyama, AkikoTanaka, Mizuki Matsuda** and **Yukiko Kamematsu** Client: **beacon communications kk**

ATTN ▶

Architectural Design
SOUTH PARK FABRICATORS
& Fabrication

San Francisco, CA
415-974-6622

Architectural Design
SOUTH PARK FABRICATORS
& Fabrication

San Francisco, CA
U.S.A.

Architectural Design
SOUTH PARK FABRICATORS
& Fabrication

San Francisco, CA
U.S.A.

Est. 1986

№ 136 South Park
SAN FRANCISCO, California 94107
T 415-974-6622
F 415-777-8633

Aija Grīna
Arhitekte

Aija Grīna
Arhitekte

Apes iela 12-19
Rīga, LV–1006
Latvija

Aija Grīna
Arhitekte

Apes iela 12-19
Rīga, LV–1006
Latvija
t. 7 55 3214

Apes iela 12-19
Rīga, LV–1006
Latvija
t. 7 55 3214

Uldis Purins (Opposite) Design Firm: **Templin Brink Design** Creative Directors: **Gaby Brink** and **Joel Templin** Designers: **Gaby Brink** and **Sallie Reynolds** Photographer: **Marko Lavrisha** Client: **Southpark Fabricators** Architecture 20.21

Design Firm: **Sheaff Dorman Purins** Art Director and Designer:

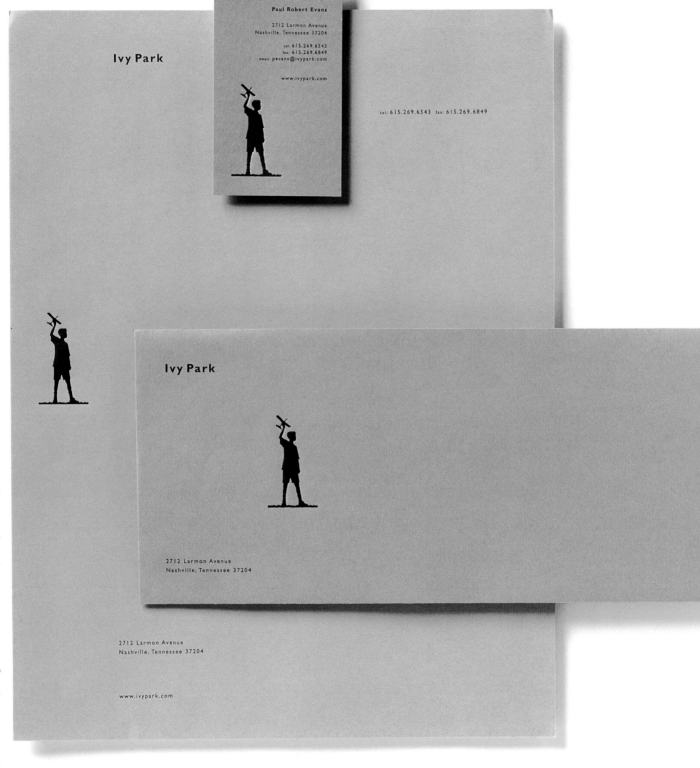

VEMAC
CAR COMPANY LIMITED

Unit 1
White Horse Business Park
Stanford-in-the-Vale
Faringdon
Oxon. SN7 8NP

Tel 01367 710 377
Fax 01367 710 219
www.vemaccars.com

With Compliments

VEMAC
CAR COMPANY LIMITED

Unit 1
White Horse Business Park
Stanford-in-the-Vale
Faringdon
Oxon. SN7 8NP

Tel 01367 710 377
Fax 01367 710 219
www.vemaccars.com

Registered in England No. 03256075
Registered Office: 18 Town Croft, Chelmsford, Essex CM1 4JX

VEMAC
CAR COMPANY LIMITED

Unit 1
White Horse Business Park
Stanford-in-the-Vale
Faringdon
Oxon. SN7 8NP

Tel 01367 710377
Fax 01367 710219
www.vemaccars.com

Chris Craft
Consultant

47 Bridge Road Hampton Court Surrey KT8 9ER
Tel: 020 8941 7557 Fax: 020 8979 3520
E-Mail:relax@inhsb.co.uk www.inhsb.co.uk

47 Bridge Road Hampton Court Surrey KT8 9ER
Tel: 020 8941 7557 Fax: 020 8979 3520
E-Mail:relax@inhsb.co.uk www.inhsb.co.uk

47 Bridge Road Hampton Court Surrey KT8 9ER Tel: 020 8941 7557 Fax: 020 8979 3520 E-Mail:relax@inhsb.co.uk www.inhsb.co.uk

Jackie Anderson
PRINCIPAL

47 Bridge Road Hampton Court Surrey KT8 9ER
Tel: 020 8941 7557 Fax: 020 8979 3520
E-Mail:relax@inhsb.co.uk www.inhsb.co.uk

47 Bridge Road Hampton Court Surrey KT8 9ER Tel: 020 8941 7557 Fax: 020 8979 3520
E-Mail:relax@inhsb.co.uk www.inhsb.co.uk

qiora

Shiseido Cosmetics (America) Ltd. 900 Third Avenue, 15th Floor New York, NY 10022-4795

qiora

535 Madison Avenue New York, NY 10022-4212

qiora

Shiseido Cosmetics (America) Ltd. 900 Third Avenue, 15th Floor New York, NY 10022-4795 Tel: 212.805.2300 Fax: 212.751.6971 www.qiora.com

Shiseido Cosmetics (America) Ltd. 900 Third Avenue, 15th Floor New York, NY 10022-4795 Tel: 212.805.2300 Fax: 212.751.6971 www.qiora.com

qiora

Karla Hekel
New Brand Administrative Manager
qiora Division

qiora

Debra Mayo
Store Manager

535 Madison Avenue
New York, NY 10022-4212
Tel: 212.527.9933
Fax: 212.527.2424
Toll free: 1.866 be qiora
E-mail: dmayo@qiora.com
www.qiora.com

BrandHarvest

1230 29th Street, NW
Washington, DC 20007

BrandHarvest

BrandHarvest

SCOTT GOLD
President & CEO

scott@brandharvest.com

Telephone 202 251 3595

Facsimile 202 965 1102

1230 29th Street, NW
Washington, DC 20007

www.brandharvest.com

Telephone 202 251 3595

Facsimile 202 965 1102

1230 29th Street, NW
Washington, DC 20007

www.brandharvest.com

Design Firm: **nickandpaul** Art Director: **Kurt Houser** Creative Director: **Paul Bennett** Designers: **Viresh Chopra** and **Micheal Choo** Client: **nickandpaul** Communications 26,27

the plant 425 West 15th Street, Chelsea Market, Floor 2R, NYC 10011

nickandpaul Nick Shore

at the plant 425 West 15th Street, Chelsea Market, NYC 10011
nick@nickandpaul.com T212.989.0868 F212.989.4012

nickandpaul

...kandpaul.com T212.989.0868 F212.989.4012

The Kenwood Group

75 Varney Place, San Francisco, CA 94107 Tel 415 957-5333 Fax 415 957-5311 www.kenwoodgroup.com

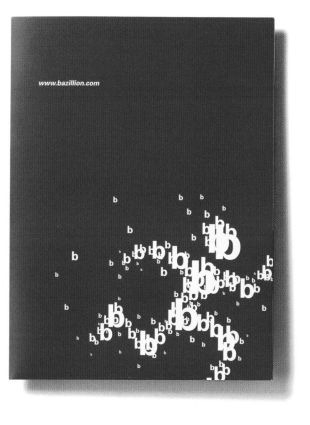

Design Firm: **The Leonhardt Group** Art Director: **Ray Ueno** Designer: **Katrin Beeck** Client: **Bazillion**

❶

step 1: cut along solid line

❷

step 2: fold along dotted line

❸

step 3: ta da!

Design Firm: **Little Fish Creative Communications** Creative Director: **Michael Donovan** Designers: **Estella Lum** and **Michael Donovan**

Communications 30,31

PARRIS
COMMUNICATIONS INC.

PARRIS
COMMUNICATIONS INC.

4739 BELLEVIEW SUITE 301
KANSAS CITY, MO 64112

PARRIS
COMMUNICATIONS INC.

4739 BELLEVIEW SUITE 301
KANSAS CITY, MO 64112
PHONE 816.931.8900
FAX 816.931.8991
WWW.PARRISCOMMUNICATIONS.COM

PUBLIC RELATIONS : MARKETING COMMUNICATIONS

PARRIS
COMMUNICATIONS INC.

PARRIS
COMMUNICATIONS INC.

PARRIS
COMMUNICATIONS INC.

Communications, Construction 32,33

Design Firm: **Hawse Design Inc.** Art Director: **Robert Hawse** Designer: **Brady Bone** Client: **Composite Resources**

Design Firm: **Fitch** Creative Directors: **Peter Chau** and **Jaimie Alexander** Designer: **Peter Chau** Photographer: **Mark Steele** Client: **Xigo**

The Loop Corporation
568 First Avenue South
Seattle, WA 98104
Telephone: 206.624.2372
Fax: 206.624.2135

The Loop Corporation
568 First Avenue South
Seattle, WA 98104
Telephone: 206.624.2372
Fax: 206.624.2135

From Jonathan Loop

The Loop Corporation
568 First Avenue South
Seattle, WA 98104

The Loop Corporation
568 First Avenue South
Seattle, WA 98104
Telephone: 206.624.2372
Fax: 206.624.2135

Jonathan Loop, President

ひめじウェルカム21実行委員会
姫 路 市 記 念 事 業 推 進 室

〒670-8501
姫 路 市 安 田 四 丁 目 1 番 地
Tel. 0792-21-2101
Fax. 0792-21-2834
URL: http://www.welcome21.co.jp
E-mail: info@welcome21.co.jp

ひめじウェルカム21実行委員会
姫 路 市 記 念 事 業 推 進 室

〒670-8501
姫 路 市 安 田 四 丁 目 1 番 地
Tel. 0792-21-2101
Fax. 0792-21-2834
URL: http://www.welcome21.co.jp
E-mail: info@welcome21.co.jp

Design Firm: **Hirano Studio Inc.** Creative and Art Director: **Keiko Hirano** Client: **Himeji Welcome 21 Executive Committee**

TIBET RUG COMPANY

STRATHMORE WRITING
25% COTTON FIBER

TIBET RUG COMPANY
1464 FOOTHILL DRIVE
SALT LAKE CITY, UT 84108

TIBET RUG COMPANY
1464 FOOTHILL DRIVE
SALT LAKE CITY, UT 84108
FAX 801 582 3501
PHONE 801 582 3334

1464 FOOTHILL DRIVE
SALT LAKE CITY, UT 84108
FAX 801 582 3501
PHONE 801 582 3334

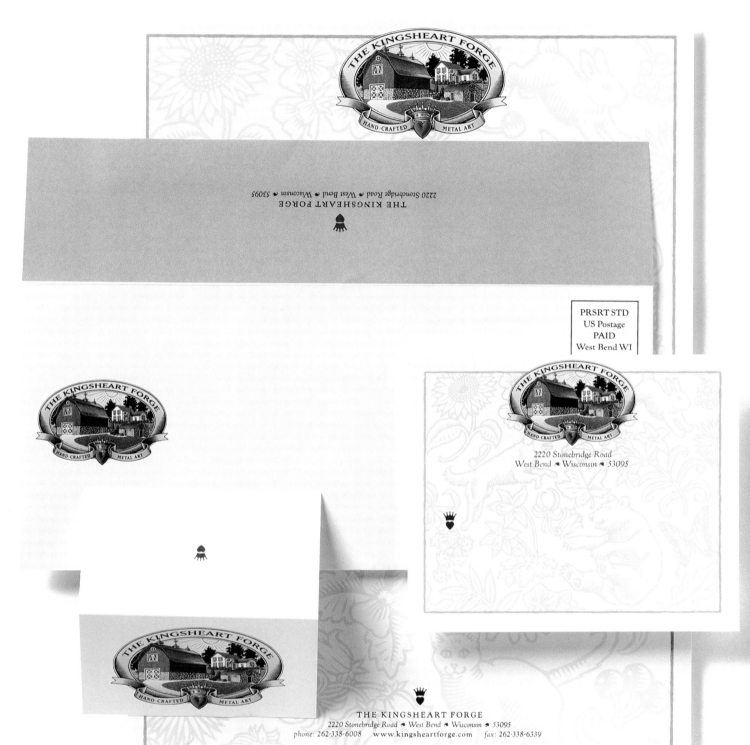

Design Firm: **Subzero Design** Art Directors and Designers: **Lee Leissring** and **Leslie Worth** Creative Director: **Lee Leissring** Illustrator: **Keith Ward** Client: **The Kingsheart Forge**

Craft 38,39

nsomnia design

603 west 13th street 1-h
austin, texas 78701

rayne
nsomniac

how do you turn
this thing off?

rayne
nsomniac

always dreaming
never sleeping

rayne
nsomniac

continuous
creative energy

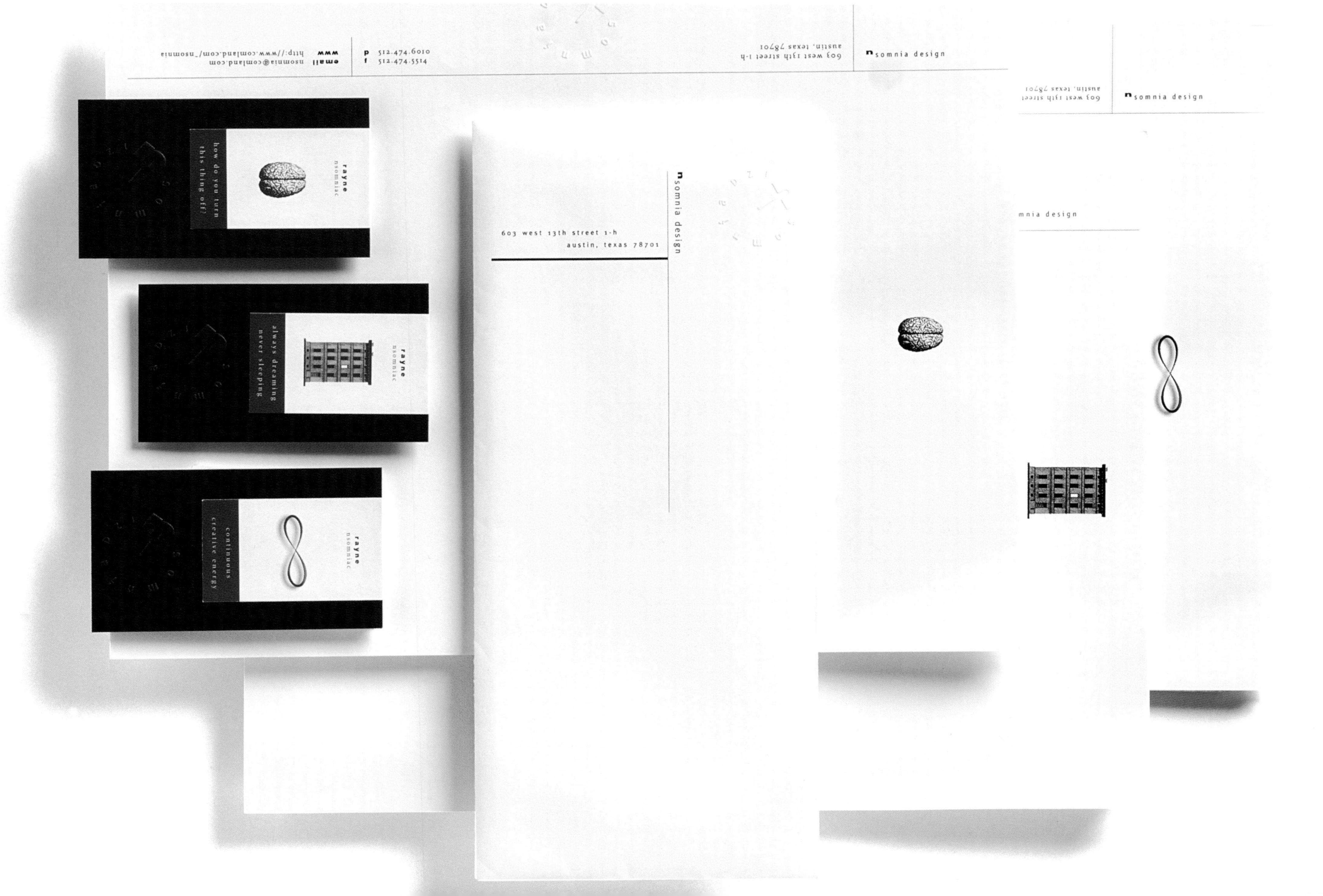

Total-løsninger for lyd, lys & scenografi – salg & utleie

tts

Tel + 47 22 38 47 47 Fax + 47

tts

Tel + 47 22 38 47 47 Fax + 47 22 38 47 48 E-mail: trollteknikk@online.no

tts

Troll teater & sceneteknikk as Nedregate 7 N-0551 Oslo

Troll teater & sceneteknikk as Nedregate 7 N-0551 Oslo

tts

Pål Ellertsen
Daglig leder/ partner

Tel + 47 22 38 47 47 Fax + 47 22 38 47 48
E-mail: trollteknikk@online.no mobil 92 80 44 54
Troll teater & sceneteknikk as Nedregate 7 N-0551 Oslo

E-mail: trollteknikk@online.no

Troll teater & sceneteknikk as Nedregate 7 N-0551 Oslo Org.nr: 977023130

Design Firm: **Rose & Hopp Design A/S** Art Directors and Designers: **Magne Hopp** and **Gina Rose** Client: **TTS**

Creative Services 40, 41

popmultimedia

popmultimedia

popmultimedia

3421 THORNDYKE AVE. W.
SEATTLE, WA 98119   www.popmultimedia.com

popmultimedia

BILL PREDMORE PRESIDENT/CEO
bill@popmultimedia.com

popmultimedia

3421 THORNDYKE AVE. W.   **TEL** 206.728.7997
SEATTLE, WA 98119   **FAX** 206.728.1144

3421 THORNDYKE AVE. W.   **TEL** 206.728.7997
SEATTLE, WA 98119   **FAX** 206.728.1144

www.popmultimedia.com

TARZAN

TARZAN

TARZAN

DANIEL FORTIN
Président
Directeur de la création

Tarzan communications inc. 20 Marie-Anne ouest, Montréal, Québec. H2W 1B5. (514) 843-5911 Fax: (514) 982-6022

Tarzan communications inc. 20 Marie-Anne ouest, Montréal, Québec. H2W 1B5

Tarzan communications inc. 20 Marie-Anne ouest, Montréal, Québec. H2W 1B5

TEL: (514) 843-5911

FAX: (514) 982-6022

Design Firm: **Tarzan Communications Inc.** Designers: **Daniel Fortin** and **George Fok** Client: **Tarzan Communications Inc.**

Creative Communications Services 42,43

ARia

Mary Boncher

Model and
Talent Management

Aria
1017 West Washington
Suite 2c
Chicago, Illinois 60607
p 312.243.9400
f 312.243.9020
www.ariamodel.com

Model and
Talent Management

Aria
1017 West Washington
Suite 2c
Chicago, Illinois 60607
p 312.243.9400
f 312.243.9020
www.ariamodel.com

Owners:
Mary Boncher
Marie Anderson Boyd

ARia

Model and
Talent Management

Aria
1017 West Washington
Suite 2c
Chicago, Illinois 60607

Design Firm: **Liska & Associates Inc.** Art Director: **Steve Liska** Designer: **Kim Fry** Client: **Aria Model & Talent Management**

marketing
and design for
Business and
Industry

www.IRIDIUM192.com

★ ★ ★ ★ ★

marketing + design for Business + Industry | **IRIDIUM**

urgent
regular

134 St.Paul Street Ottawa Ontario CANADA K1L 8E4

DELIVER TO

marketing
and design for
Business and
Industry

www.IRIDIUM192.com

marketing
and design for
Business and
Industry

www.IRIDIUM192.com

marketing + design for Busin

613 748.3336 ~ vox
748.3372 ~ fax

tawa Ontario CANADA K1L 8E4

statement | news release

Design Firm: **The Leonhardt Group** Art Director: **Steve Watson** Creative Director: **Lesley Feldman** Client: **Headstrong**

Creative Services 46, 47 · Design Firm: **Hornall Anderson Design Works Inc.** Designers: **Jack Anderson, Lisa Cerveny, Don Stayner** and **Mary Chin Hutchison** Client: **Twelve Horses**

Callaghan Potter Letellier
Facility Planners

Jim Potter B.E.S. (Architecture)

211-2141 Thurston Drive
Ottawa Ontario K1G 6C9
T 613-739-3699
F 613-739-3965
E jim@cpldesign.on.ca

Callaghan Potter Letellier
Design Consultants Inc.

211-2141 Thurston Drive Ottawa Ontario K1G 6C9
T 613-739-3699 F 613-739-3965 E info@cpldesign.on.ca

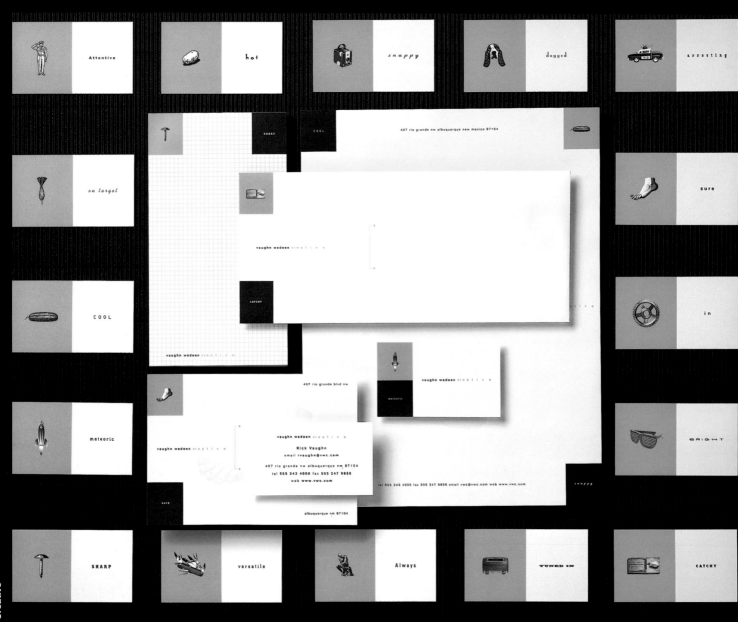

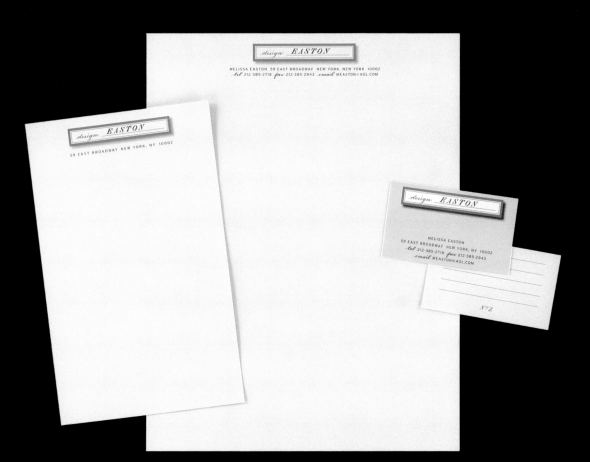

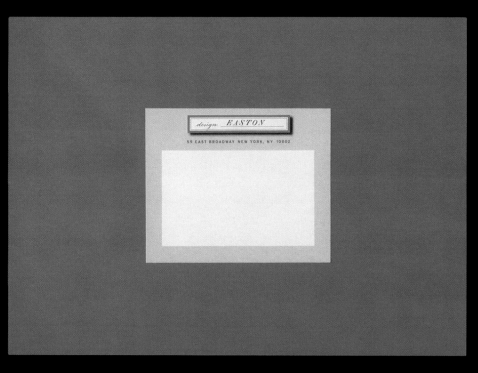

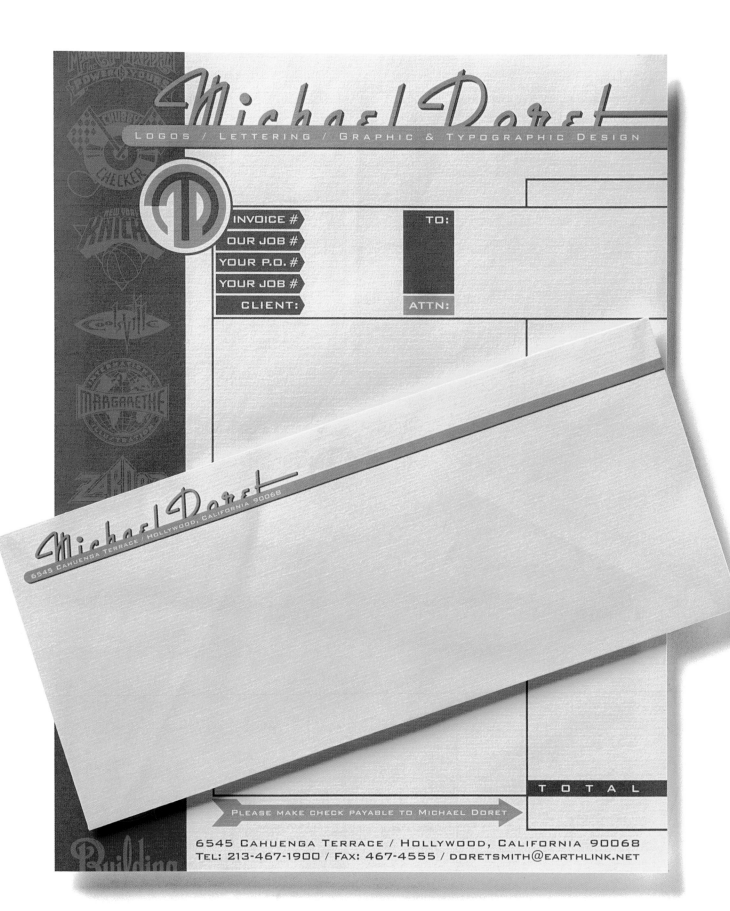

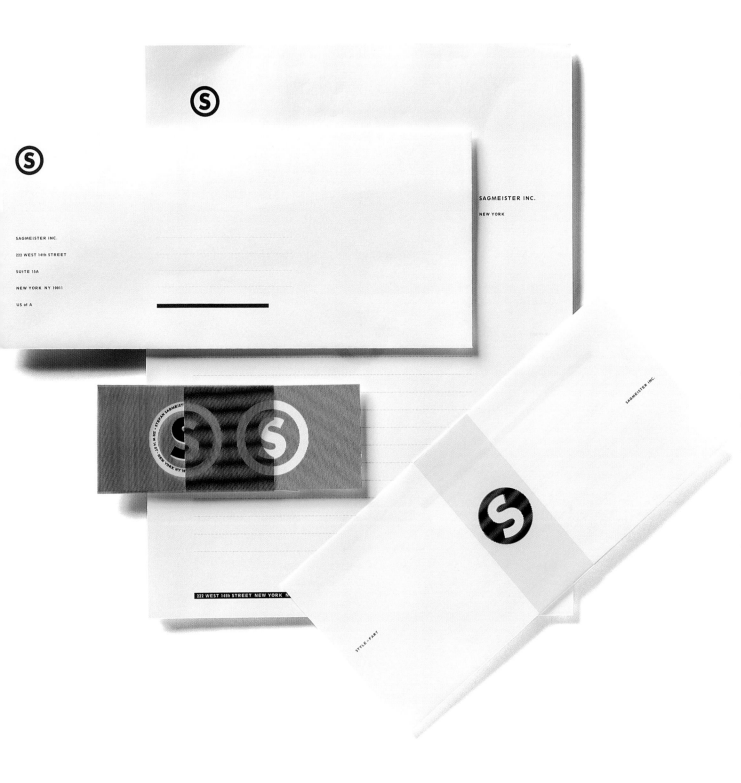

MICHAEL SCHWAB
415.257.5792

MICHAEL SCHWAB STUDIO

108 TAMALPAIS AVENUE   SAN ANSELMO, CA 94960   415.257.5792   FAX 257.5793

A DIVISION OF ANGELS • COWBOYS, INC.

...rgia 30318

EGO

SIMPLE

Context alters meaning.

Context alters meaning.

Context alters meaning.

Context alters meaning.

Context alters meaning.

Context alters meaning.

Context alters meaning.

Context alters meaning.

JUDG

EXTR

Context alters meaning.

EAI®

Goose Black Labrador Retriever
887 West Marietta St. NW J-101 Atlanta, Georgia 30318
404 875 8225 fax 875 4402

TANGO+

Tango Design
Newcombe House
45 Notting Hill Gate
London W11 3LQ

Tel: +44 (0)207 569 5757
Fax: +44 (0)207 569 5656
ISDN +44 (0)207 569 5799
Web: www.tangodesign.com

Tango Design Newcombe House 45 Notting Hill Gate London W11 3LQ Tel: +44 (0)207 569 5757 Fax: +44 (0)207 569 5656 ISDN +44 (0)20 7792 2295

Tango Design is a trading name of Identica Limited

TANGO+

TANGO+

Tango Design Newcombe House 45 Notting Hill Gate London W11 3LQ

Tel: +44 (0)207 569 5757 Fax: +44 (0)207 569 5656

Email: tango@tangodesign.com

Tango Design is a trading name of Identica Limited

The Identica Partnership
Identica Limited Registered in England No. 2872075.
Registered Address: Finsgate 5-7 Cranwood Street
London EC1V 9EE. VAT Registration No. 672 2020 69.
The Identica Partnership & Tango Design are trading
names of Identica Limited.

Letterhead 300FeetOut

pier 9
suite
114
san
fran
cisco
ca
94111

www.300FeetOut.com

Envelope 300FeetOut

pier 9
suite
114
san
fran
cisco
ca
94111

pier 9
suite
114
san
fran
cisco
ca
94111

BusinessCard 300FeetOut

www.300FeetOut.com

tel 415 477 9940
fax 415 477 9946

Design Firm: **300 Feet Out** Art Director: **Ryan Michell** Creative Director: **Nina Dietzel** Designer: **Anna Beruander** Client: **300 Feet Out**

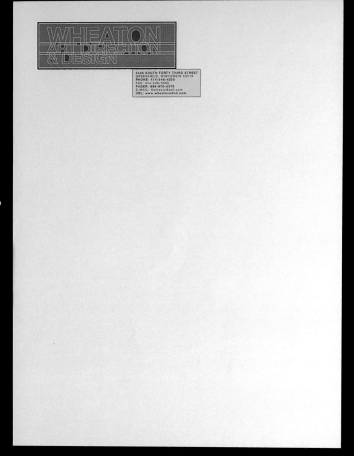

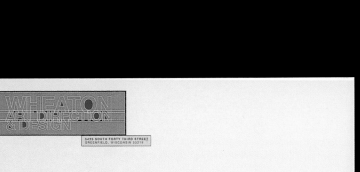

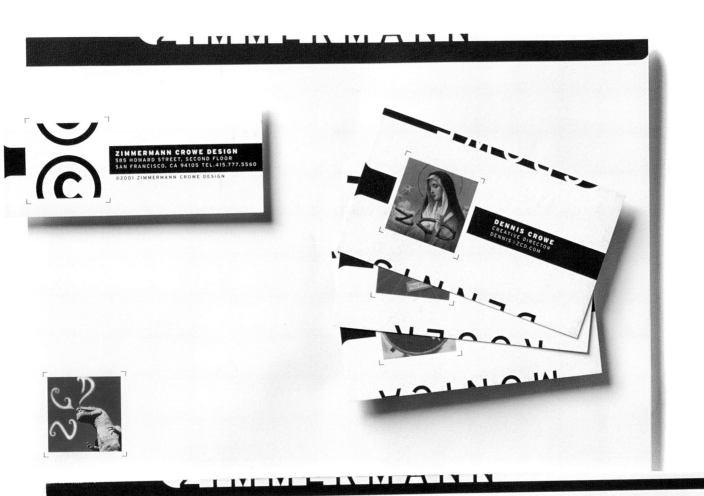

WILLIAMS
MURRAY
HAMM

CREATING DIFFERENCE
Williams Murray Hamm The Heals Building, Alfred Mews, London W1P 9LB
Tel +44 (0)20 7255 3232 Fax +44 (0)20 7637 8404 wmh@creatingdifference.com

WHIZZ
MAIL
HERE

CREATING DIFFERENCE
Williams Murray Hamm The Heals Building, Alfred Mews, London W1P 9LB
Tel +44 (0)20 7255 3232 Fax +44 (0)20 7637 8404 wmh@creatingdifference.com

Registered in England No 3305951, Registered Office Greenwood House, 4-7 Salisbury Court, London EC4Y 8BT

WELL-SPOKEN
MILD
HONEY

CLARE POUPARD
Williams Murray Hamm The Heals Building, Alfred Mews, London W1P 9LB
Tel +44 (0)20 7255 3232 Fax +44 (0)20 7637 8404
clarep@creatingdifference.com ISDN +44 (0)20 7636 4593

Rose & Hopp Design as Briskebyveien 72 N-0259 Oslo Tel +4722562025 Fax +4722562023 e-mail:rosehopp@rosehopp.no [org.nr: 965916156]

ROSE+HOPP DESIGN

Rose & Hopp Design as Briskebyveien 72 N-0259 Oslo Fax +4722562023
Tel +4722562025 Mobil 90982476 e-mail:rosehopp@rosehopp.no

Magne Hopp
grafisk designer/partner

ROSE+HOPP DESIGN

Rose & Hopp Design as Briskebyveien 72 N-0259 Oslo e-mail:rosehopp@rosehopp.no

ROSE+HOPP DESIGN

Design Firm: **Rose & Hopp Design A/S** Art Directors and Designers: **Magne Hopp** and **Gina Rose** Photographer: **Tommy Norman Hansen** Client: **Rose & Hopp Design A/S**   Design 62,63

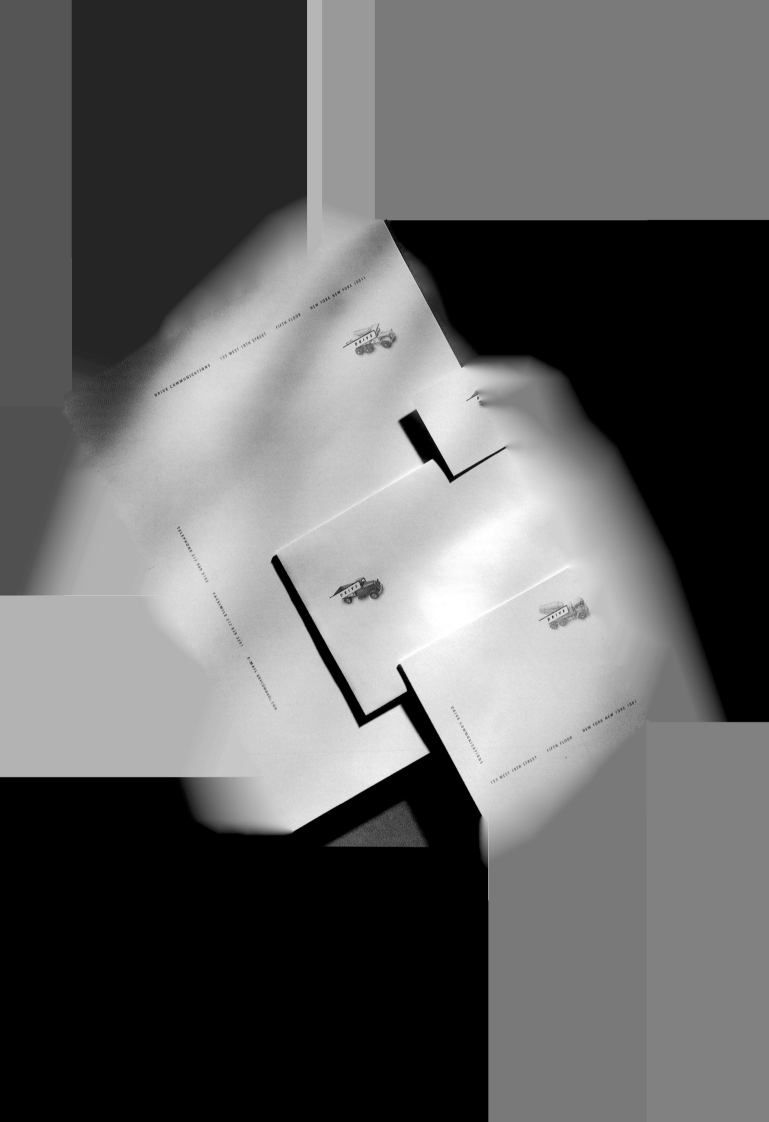

Design Firm: **Designworks** Art Director: **Debbie Feasey** Designers: **Aaron Pollock** and **Jeff Johnson** Client: **Designworks**

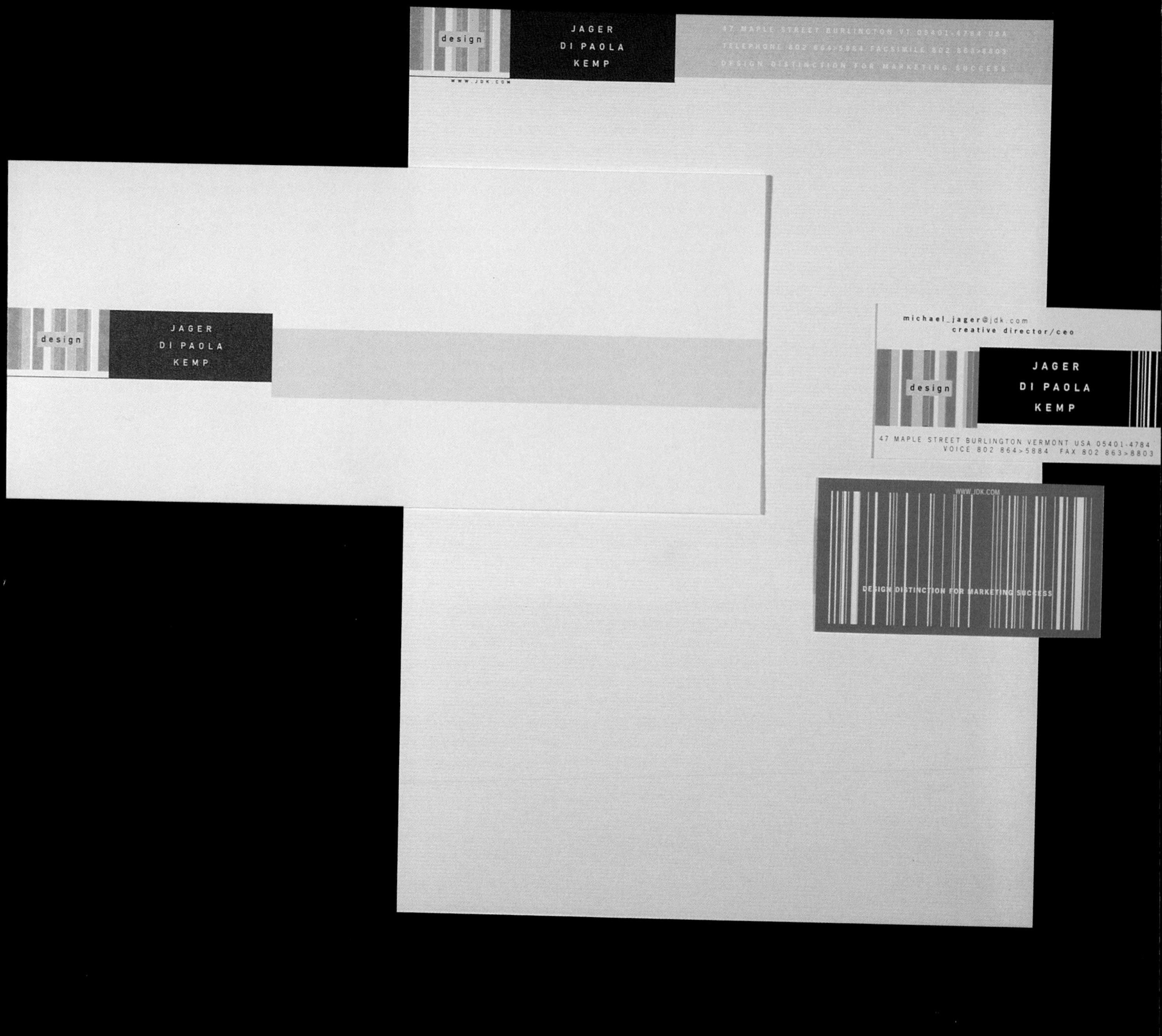

Design Firm: **Jager Di Paola Kemp** Creative Director: **Michael Jager** Designer: **David Covell** Client: **Jager Di Paola Kemp**

storm visual communications inc.

70 George Street, 3rd floor
Ottawa, Ontario K1N 5V9
www.storm.on.ca

telephone 613.789.0244
facsimile   613.789.0265

storm visual communications inc.

70 George Street, 3rd floor
Ottawa, Ontario K1N 5V9
www.storm.on.ca

telephone 613.789.0244
facsimile   613.789.0265

Design Firm: **Storm Visual Communications** Creative Director: **Robert Smith** Designers: **Kevin Kelly** and **Robert Smith** Photographer: **Headlight Innovative Imagery** Client: **Storm Visual Communications**   Design 66,67

〒104-0041
東京都中央区新富1-3-11銀座ビル7階

株式会社パブログラフィス圖庵

tel. 03-3537-0845 fax. 03-3537-0846
e-mail. zuan@aqua.famille.ne.jp

PABLOGRAPHIS

zuan

新谷秀実
Hidemi Shingai

PABLOGRAPHIS

zuan

Design Firm: **Pablographis Zuan** Creative Director: **Mitsuhisa Kageyama** Art Director and Designer: **Hidemi Shingai** Client: **Pablographis Zuan**

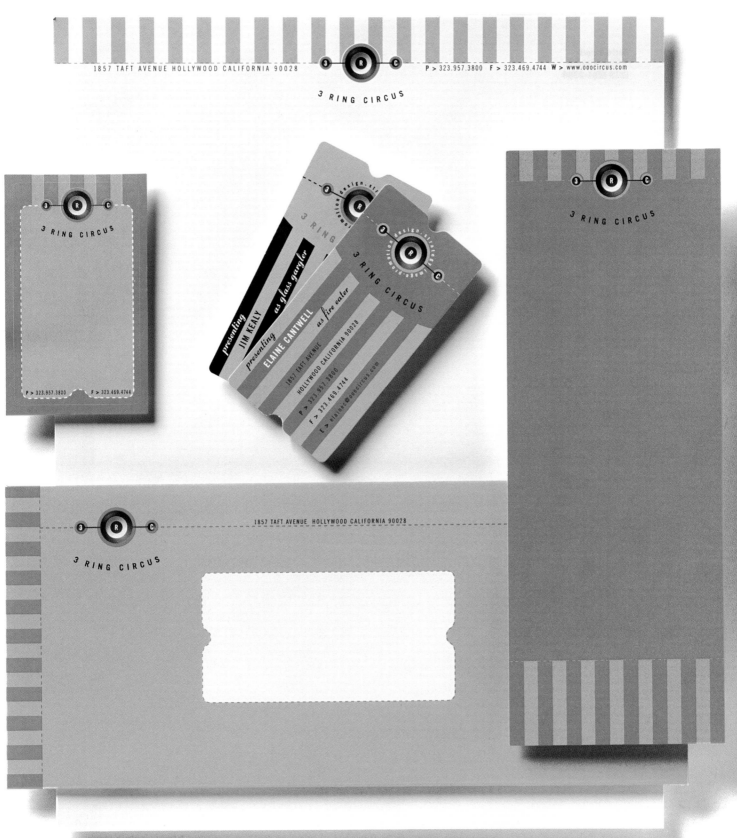

Design Firm: **3 Ring Circus** Creative Directors: **Elaine Cantwell** and **Jim Kealy** Designer: **Ania Hoffman** Client: **3 Ring Circus**   Design 68,69

Design Firm: **Cross Colours** Art Director and Designer: **Joanina Pastoll** Illustrators: **Mark Day** and **Peter Simpson** Client: **Cross Colours**

A/3

159 w pierpont ave
salt lake city, ut 84101
phone 801 521 2900
fax 801 521 2970

A/3

159 w pierpont ave
salt lake city, ut 84101

A/3

A/3

adrian pulfer

159 w pierpont ave   context / content / image
salt lake city, ut 84101
phone 801 521 2900
fax 801 521 2970

context / content / image

context / content / image

Designers: **Adrian Pulfer** and **Ganace Pulfer** Client: **A/3**

BRADBURY DESIGN INC.

Creative, Effective & Appropriate
Graphic Design Solutions

#330-1933 8th Avenue
Regina, Canada S4R 1E9

BRADBURY DESIGN INC.

Creative, Effective & Appropriate Graphic Design Solutions

P: (306) 525 4043   Toll Free: 1 800 254 7989   F: (306) 525 4068

#330-1933 8th Avenue Regina, Canada S4R 1E9   E: ideas@bradburydesign.com   W: www.bradburydesign.com

Design Firm: **Bradbury Design Inc.** Art Director, Creative Director and Designer: **Catharine Bradbury** Client: **Bradbury Design Inc.**

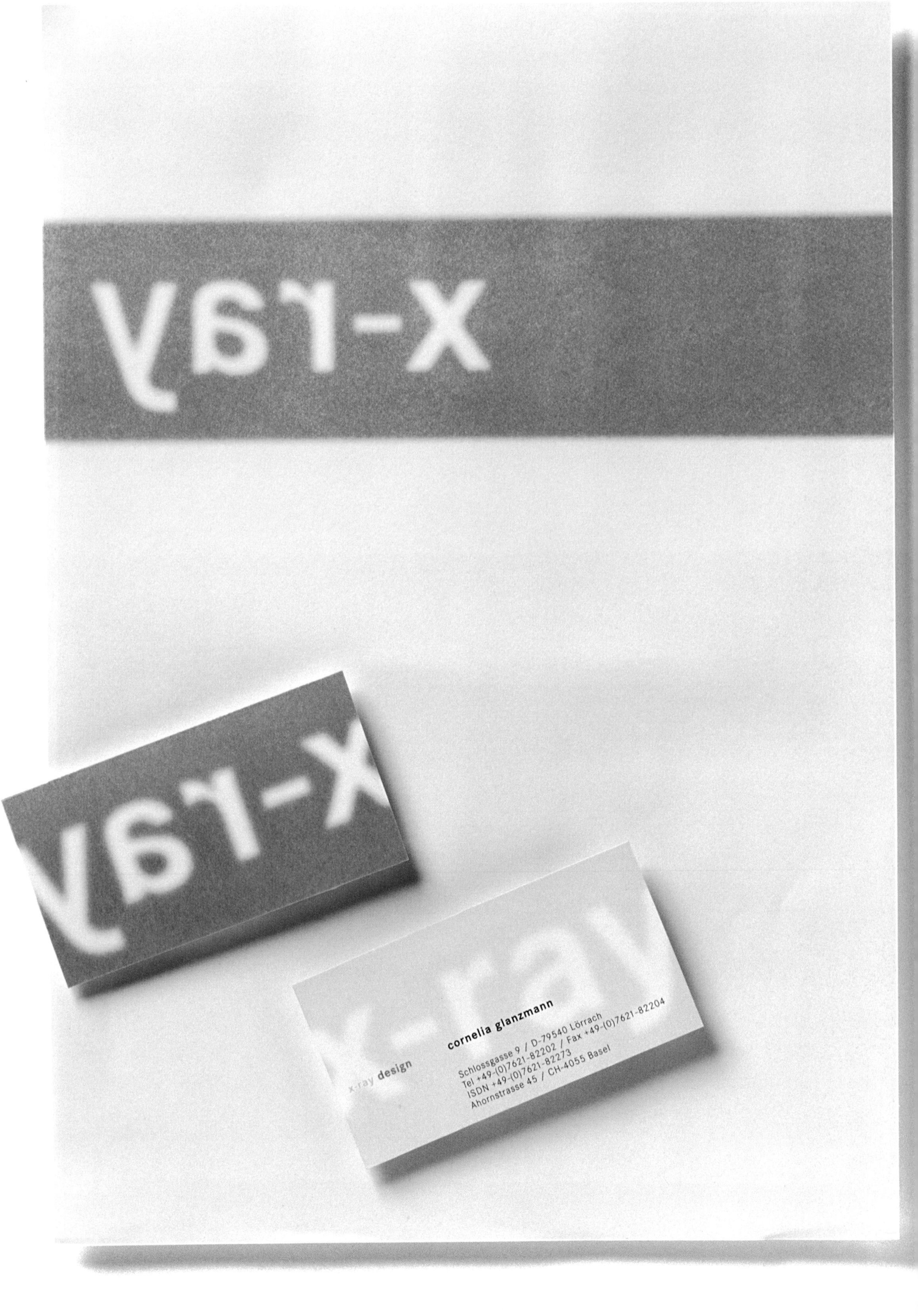

cornelia glanzmann

x-ray design

Schlossgasse 9 / D-79540 Lörrach
Tel +49-(0)7621-82202 / Fax +49-(0)7621-82204
ISDN +49-(0)7621-82273
Ahornstrasse 45 / CH-4055 Basel

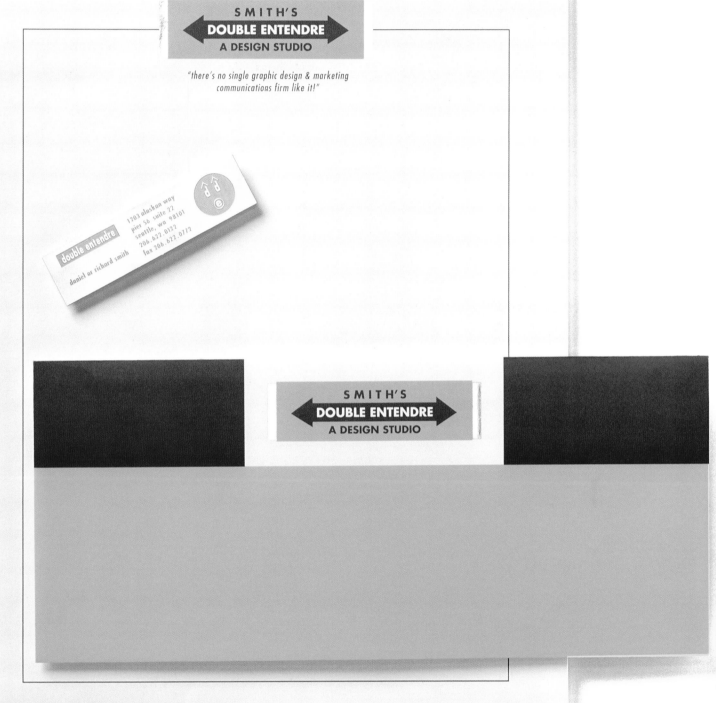

Design Firm: **double entendre** Designers: **Richard A. Smith** and **Daniel P. Smith** Client: **double entendre**

Roslyn **Eskind Associates Limited**

Christine Slobodian, AOCA

tel 416 504 6075
fax 416 504 6085
email christi@roslyneskind.com

Graphic Design @ 471 Richmond Street West 2nd fl
Consultants   Toronto, Ontario   M5V 1X9

Roslyn **Eskind Associates Limited**

Roslyn **Eskind Associates Limited**

Eskind

Associates

Limited

@

471 Richmond Street West Suite 200
Toronto, Ontario M5V 1X9

Graphic Design
Consultants

Roslyn **Eskind Associates Limited**

@

471 Richmond Street West Suite 200
Toronto, Ontario M5V 1X9

tel   416 504 6075
fax   416 504 6085
email @roslyneskind.com

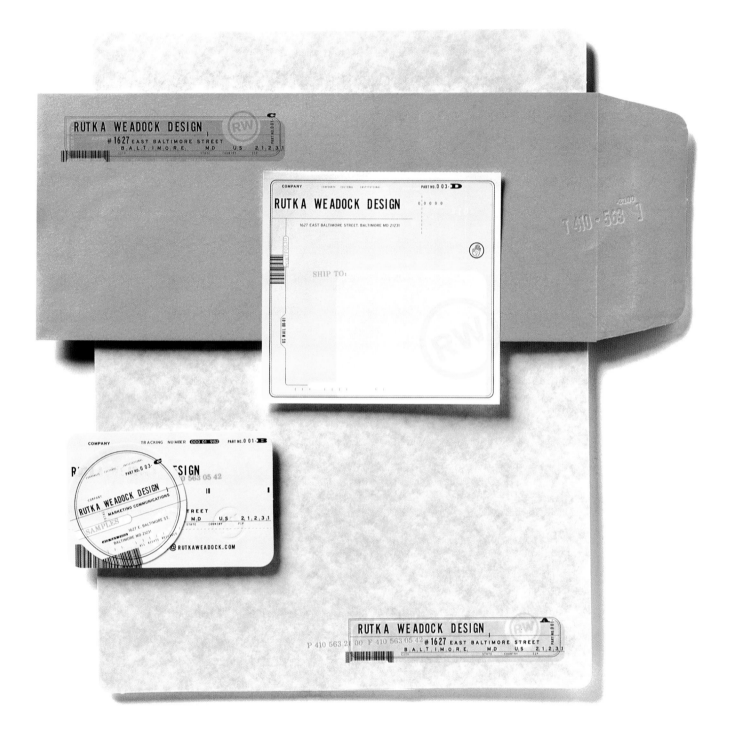

Design Firm: **Rutka Weadock Design** Art Director: **Anthony Rutka** Designer: **Darina Geiling** Client: **Rutka Weadock Design** Design 76,77

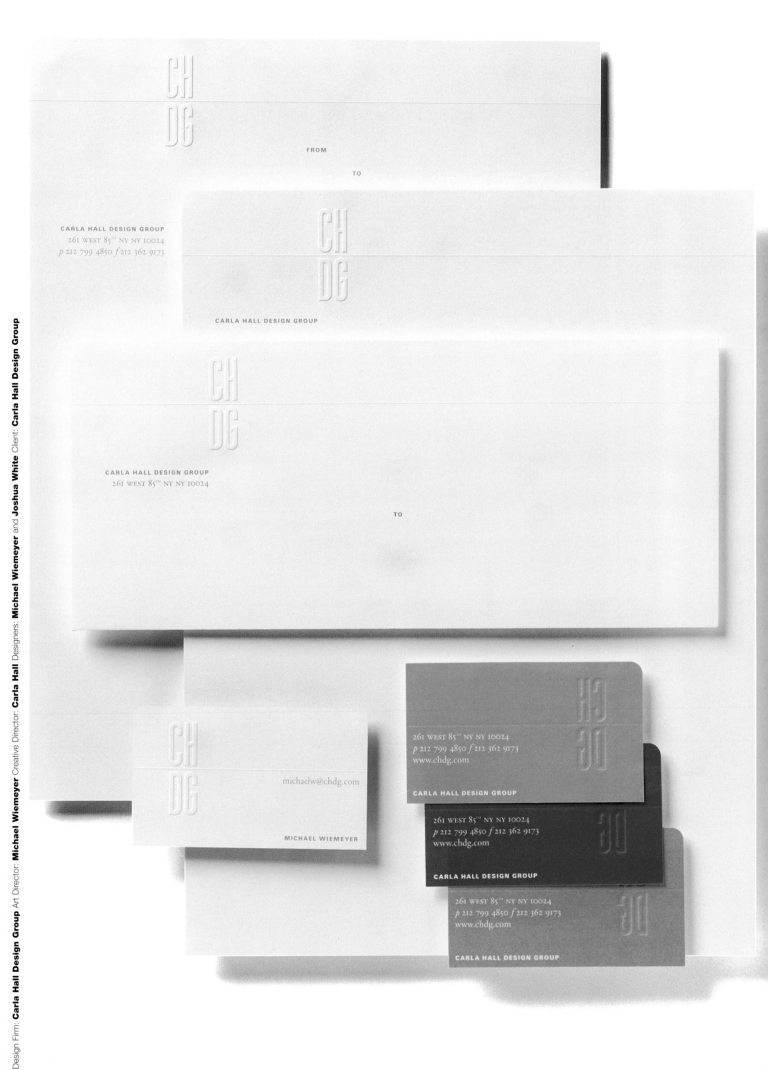

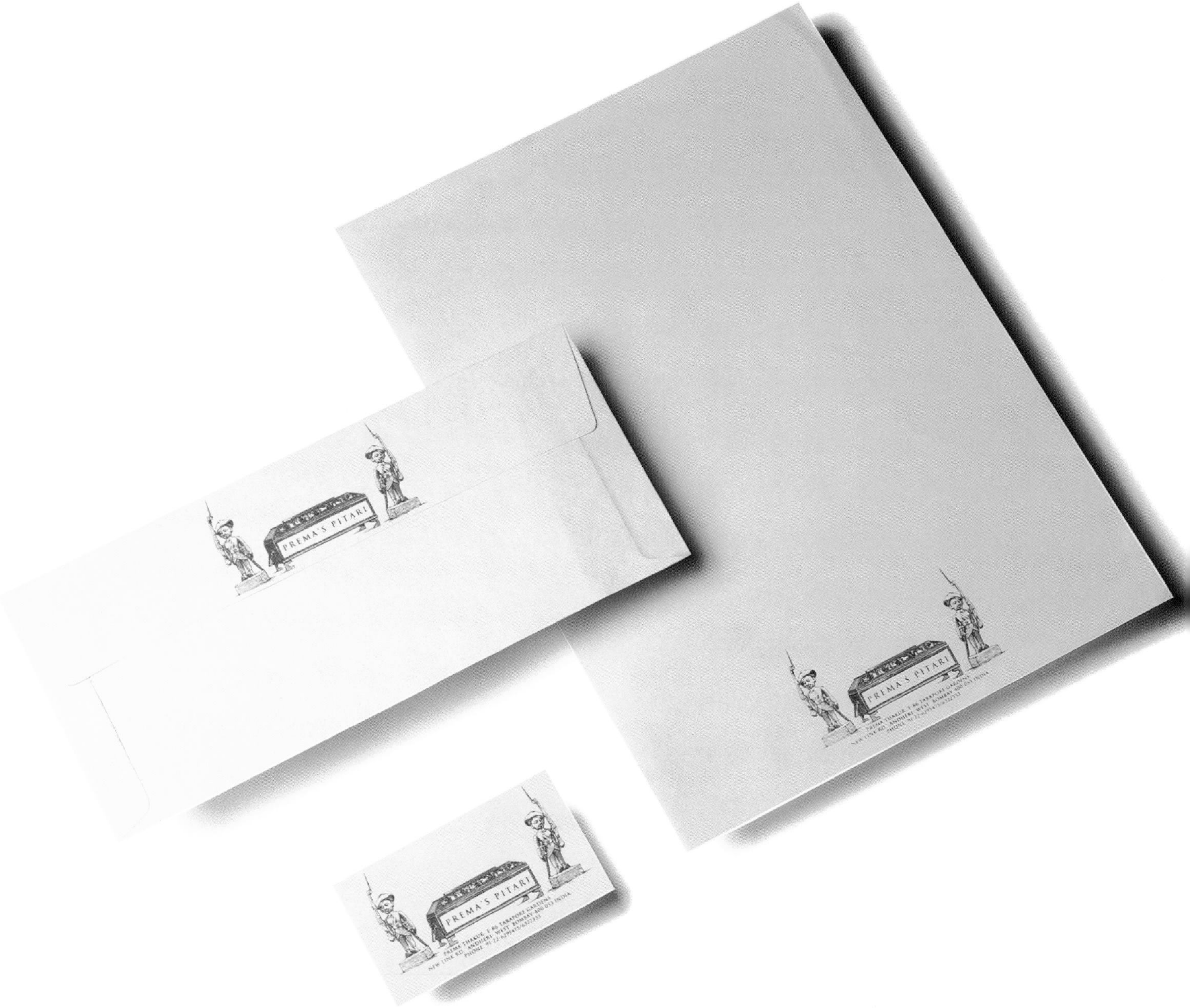

Design Firm: **Design Temple** Art Director and Designer: **Divya Thakur** Illustrator: **Sanjay Shetye** Client: **Prema's Pitari**

Design Firm: **Scandinavian Design Group** Creative Director: **Gary Swindell** Designers: **Adam Cable** and **Marc Ligeti** Client: **Scandinavian Design Group**

KATE PEEPLES
DIRECTOR OF PUBLIC RELATIONS
AND MARKETING

MAYMONT
1700 HAMPTON ST. RICHMOND, VA 23220
TEL. 804.358.7166 EXT. 316 FAX. 804.358.9994

MAYMONT
1700 HAMPTON STREET RICHMOND, VA 23220
TEL. 804.358.7166 FAX. 804.358.9994 THE MAYMONT HOUSE,
THE NATURE CENTER, WILDLIFE PARK, CHILDREN'S PARK,
ARBORETUM, THE CARRIAGE COLLECTION, FORMAL GARDENS

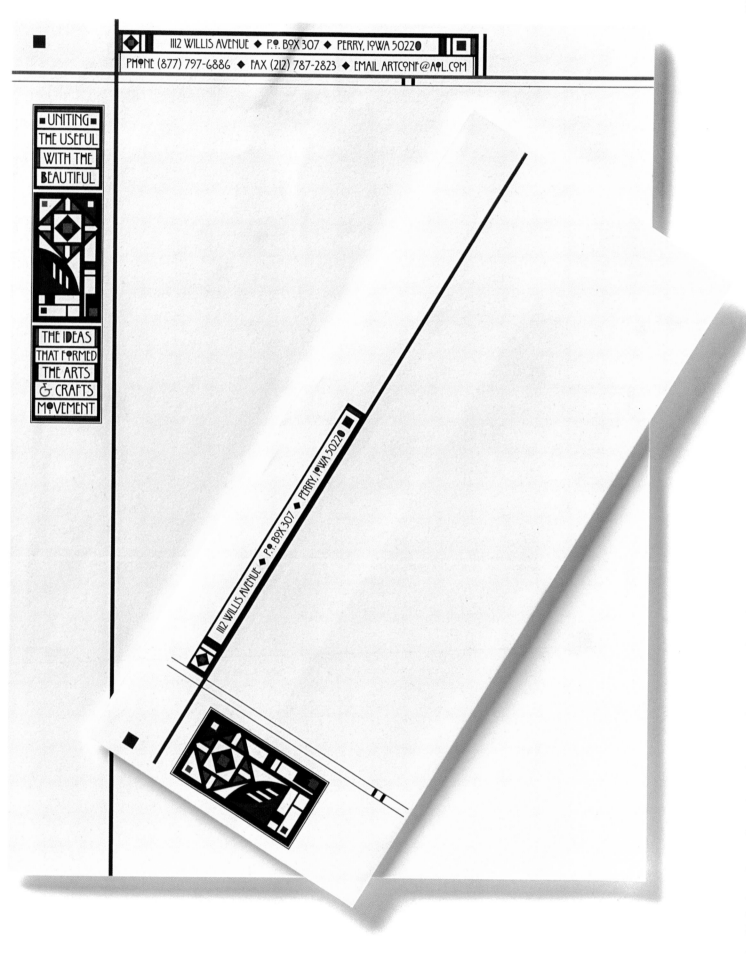

1112 WILLIS AVENUE ◆ P.O. BOX 307 ◆ PERRY, IOWA 50220

PHONE (877) 797-6886 ◆ FAX (212) 787-2823 ◆ EMAIL ARTCONF@AOL.COM

UNITING
THE USEFUL
WITH THE
BEAUTIFUL

THE IDEAS
THAT FORMED
THE ARTS
& CRAFTS
MOVEMENT

1112 WILLIS AVENUE ◆ P.O. BOX 307 ◆ PERRY, IOWA 50220

PET FAIR

645 Southcenter Mall
Suite #341
Seattle, WA 98188
(206) 539-4524

Timothy Enarson, Event Coordinator

645 Southcenter Mall
Suite #341
Seattle, WA 98188
(206) 539-4524

PET FAIR

645 Southcenter Mall • Suite #341 • Seattle, WA 98188

PET FAIR

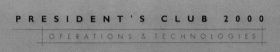

PRESIDENT'S CLUB 2000
OPERATIONS & TECHNOLOGIES

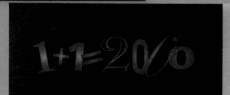

PRESIDENT'S CLUB 2000
RETAIL MARKETS

Design Firm: **Vaughn Wedeen Creative** Art Directors: **Pamela Chang** and **Rick Vaughn** Creative Directors: **Pamela Chang** and **Foster Hurley** Designer: **Pamela Chang** Copywriter: **Foster Hurley** Client: **US West** (opposite) Client: **Pet Fair** Events 86, 87

JUDITH HAARMANN

ELBCHAUSSEE 16 22765 HAMBURG
TEL/FAX 0049 (0)40 39900694

JUDITH HAARMANN

ELBCHAUSSEE 16 22765 HAMBURG
TEL/FAX 0049 (0)40 39900694
BERSENBRÜCKER SPARKASSE
KTO-NR 118786086 BLZ 26551540

Amy Coe Inc.

578 Post Road East #506

Westport, Connecticut 06880

T 203.221.3050 F 203.221.3051

Amy Coe Inc.

578 Post Road East #506

Westport, Connecticut 06880

T 203.221.3050 F 203.221.3051

Design Firm: **nickandpaul** Creative Director: **Nin Glaister** Designers: **Amy Nadaskay** and **Danielle Stella** Client: **Amy Coe**

annascholz

Unit 9. 81 Southern Row
London W10 5AL
Great Britain
T+44(0)181 964 3040
F+44(0)181 964 5020
E-mail ascholz@dircon.co.uk

annascholz

Unit 9. 81 Southern Row London W10 5AL Great Britain T+44(0)181 964 3040 F+44(0)181 964 5020

annascholz

ANNI KUAN

242 W 38TH ST NEW YORK NY 10018 PHONE 212 704 4038 FAX 704 0651

Art Director: **Stefan Sagmeister** Designers: **Hjalti Karlsson** and **Stefan Sagmeister** Client: **Anni Kuan Design**

■I F A X

G Ö T Z

Von :

An :

Firma :

Datum :

Betreff :

Seiten :

▶ D A Y 4 N I G H T W E A R I N N O V A T I O N

GÖTZ MODE GMBH & CO. KG │ Dorfstraße 58 · 72459 Albstadt-Margrethausen · Postfach 10 02 09 · 72423 Albstadt
Telefon 0 74 31/7 00-0 · Telefax 0 74 31/7 00-1 55 · Homepage www.goetz-mode.de · E-Mail info@goetz-mode.de

G Ö T Z

▲ D A Y & N I G H T W E A R I N N O V A T I O N

LICENCE

GÖTZBURG

GÖTZ MADE IN QUALITY

margret

SINCE 1889

GÖTZ MODE GMBH & CO. KG | Dorfstraße 58 · 72459 Albstadt-Margrethausen · Postfach 10 02 09 · 72423 Albstadt
Telefon 0 74 31/7 00-0 · Telefax 0 74 31/7 00-1 55 · Homepage www.goetz-mode.de · E-Mail info@goetz-mode.de
Rechtsform: Kommanditgesellschaft · Sitz Albstadt · Registergericht Albstadt HRA 207 Persönlich haftende
Gesellschafterin: GÖTZ MODE VERWALTUNGS GMBH · Sitz: Albstadt · Registergericht: Albstadt HRB 941
Geschäftsführer: Gregor Götz · Thomas Götz · Wolfram Stegmaier

JOHN NELS HATLEBERG

1016 FIFTH AVENUE NEW YORK NY 10028

TELEPHONE 212.779.7931 FAX 212.879.0476

E-MAIL BIGGEMS@EARTHLINK.NET

JOHN NELS HATLEBERG

1016 FIFTH AVENUE NEW YORK NY 10028

JOHN NELS HATLEBERG

1016 FIFTH AVENUE NEW YORK NY 10028

TELEPHONE 212.779.7931 FAX 212.879.0476

E-MAIL BIGGEMS@EARTHLINK.NET

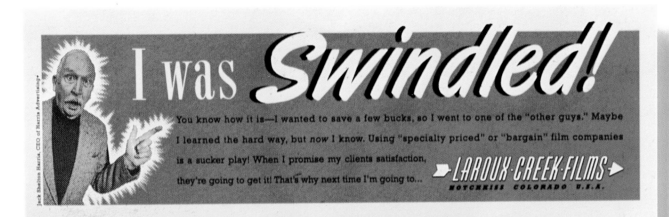

I was *Swindled!*

You know how it is—I wanted to save a few bucks, so I went to one of the "other guys." Maybe I learned the hard way, but *now* I know. Using "specialty priced" or "bargain" film companies is a sucker play! When I promise my clients satisfaction, they're going to get it! That's why next time I'm going to...

Jack Shelton Harris, CEO of Harris Advertising

LAROUX·CREEK·FILMS
HOTCHKISS COLORADO U.S.A.

1462 2800 RD. ZIP CODE: 81419
LAROUX CREEK FILMS
#4-60 · HOTCHKISS, COLORADO · U.S.A.

STAMP

fx-111

Morty Baran
Laroux Creek Films
Friends, you can reach us at:
**1462 2800 Road
Hotchkiss, Colorado
Our Zip Code: 81419
Phone: (970) 835-3909
Fax: (970) 835-4209**

The best
in the
industry—
Give us a call
today!

Laroux Creek Films
LCF

D-12

**LAROUX
Creek Films**

No obligation! Send
today for information
about the fool-proof
work of Laroux Creek
Films and how they
assure you perfect
production. D-12

We're
standing
by—
Mail coupon
today!

Send to: Laroux Creek Films, 1462 2800 Rd. Hotchkiss, CO Zip Code: 81419 Phone: (970) 835-3909 *or fax it to this number:* (970) 835-4209. We're waiting to hear from you! We shoot in color!

( ) Please send me info. giving me complete details on Laroux Creek Films. No salesman is to call. Soon the work will be paying for itself in profits!

( ) Don't send me anything. I'm quite happy losing profits and clients, and I don't want to advance in the field.

NAME
COMPANY
ADDRESS
CITY
ZONE
STATE
ZIP

Laroux Creek Films
LCF

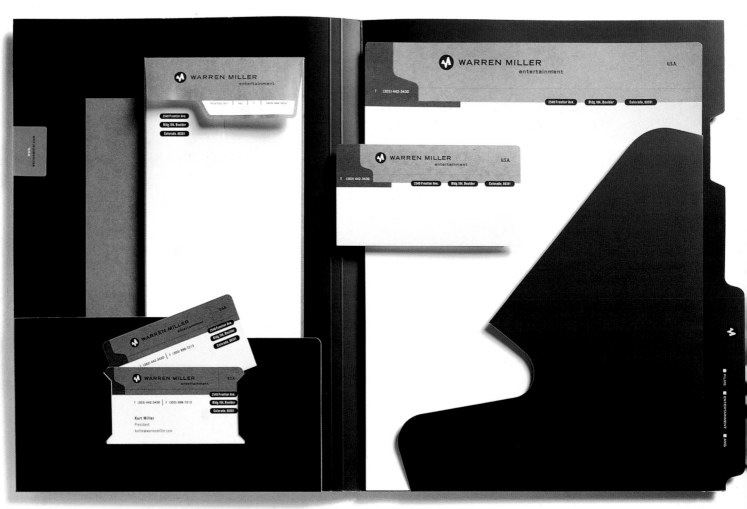

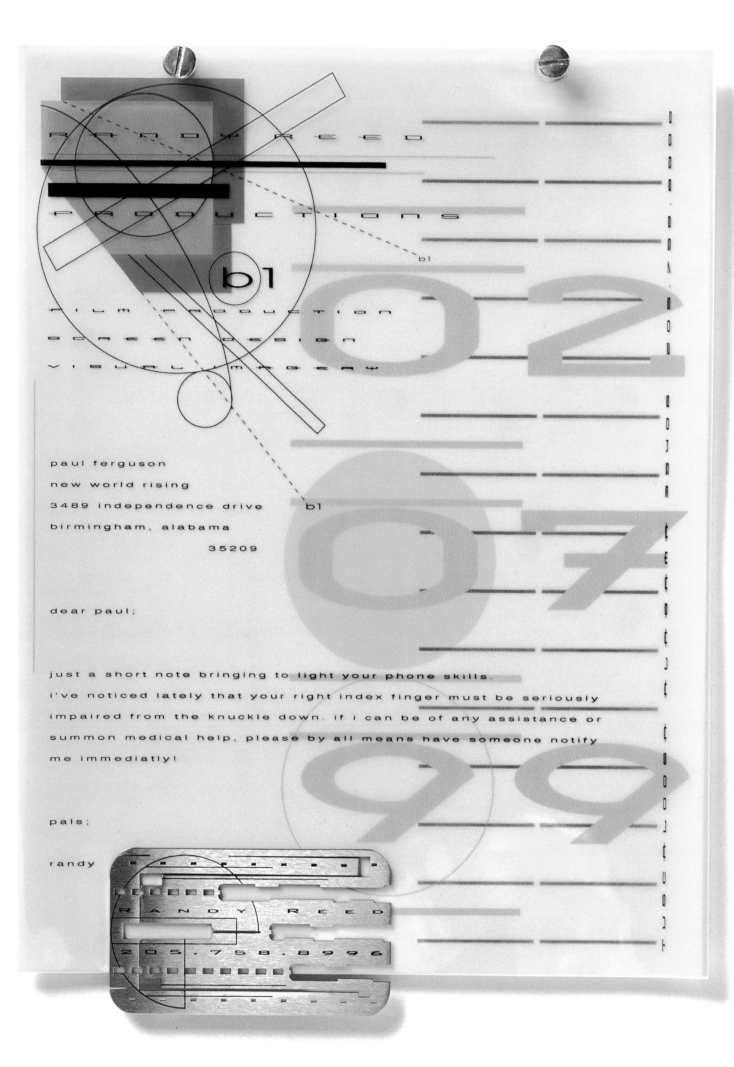

RANDY REED

PRODUCTIONS

b1

FILM PRODUCTION
SCREEN DESIGN
VISUAL IMAGERY

paul ferguson
new world rising
3489 independence drive
birmingham, alabama
35209

dear paul;

just a short note bringing to light your phone skills.
i've noticed lately that your right index finger must be seriously
impaired from the knuckle down. if i can be of any assistance or
summon medical help, please by all means have someone notify
me immediatly!

pals;

randy

RANDY REED

205.758.8996

Slavin Schaffer Films

62 Greene Street
New York City
10012

Telephone
212.925.8167
Facsimile
212.966.2866

E-mail
info@slavinschaffer.com

Slavin Schaffer Films

62 Greene Street
New York City 10012

Telephone 212.925.8167
Facsimile 212.966.2866

E-mail
info@slavinschaffer.com

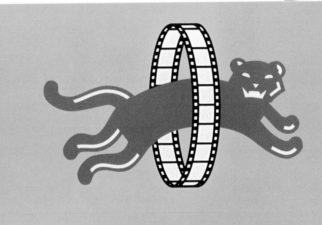

Slavin Schaffer Films

Slavin Schaffer Films

62 Greene Street
New York City 10012

Design Firm: **Susan Hochbaum Design** Art Directors: **Susan Hochbaum** and **Steven Guarnaccia** Designer: **Susan Hochbaum** Illustrator: **Steven Guarnaccia** Client: **Slavin Schaffer Films**   Film 98,99

DAVID BINDER PRODUCTIONS 39 WEST 14TH STREET #504
NEW YORK, NY 10011 *[212] 691-7131 FAX [212] 741-9170*
DAVID@DAVIDBINDERPRODUCTIONS.COM

DAVID BINDER PRODUCTIONS 39 WEST 14TH STREET #504
NEW YORK, NY 10011 *[212] 691-7131 FAX [212] 741-9170*
DAVID@DAVIDBINDERPRODUCTIONS.COM

DAVID BINDER PRODUCTIONS 39 WEST 14TH STREET #504
NEW YORK, NY 10011

DAVID BINDER PRODUCTIONS 39 WEST 14TH STREET #504
NEW YORK, NY 10011 *[212] 691-7131 FAX [212] 741-9170*
DAVID@DAVIDBINDERPRODUCTIONS.COM

DAVID BINDER PRODUCTIONS 39 WEST 14TH STREET #504
NEW YORK, NY 10011 *[212] 691-7131 FAX [212] 741-9170*
DAVID@DAVIDBINDERPRODUCTIONS.COM

DAVID BINDER PRODUCTIONS 39 WEST 14TH STREET #504
NEW YORK, NY 10011 *[212] 691-7131 FAX [212] 741-9170*
DAVID@DAVIDBINDERPRODUCTIONS.COM

(previous spread) Design Firm: **Studio d Design** Art Director and Designer: **Laurie Demartino** Photographer: **Steve Belkowitz** Client: **Belkowitz Photography & Film** (this page) Design Firm: **Stone Yamashita** Art Director and Designer: **Jennifer Olsen** Client: **David Binder Productions**

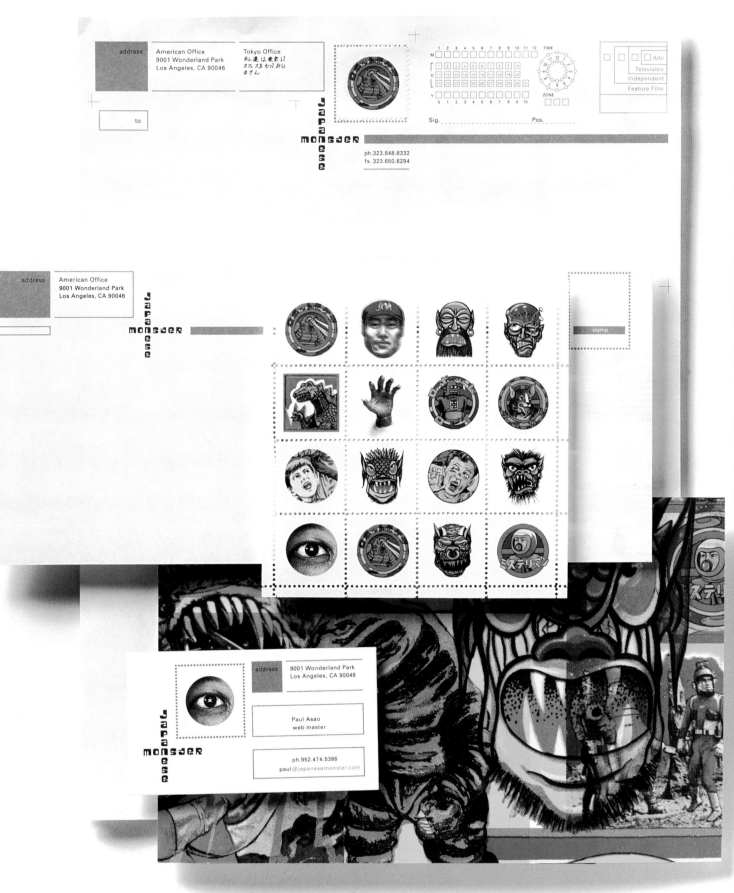

Design Firm: **Charles S. Anderson Design** Art Directors: **Charles S. Anderson** and **Todd Piper-Hauswirth** Designer: **Todd Piper-Hauswirth** Photographer: **Mr. French Printstock** Client: **Japanese Monster**

INDEPENDENT

777 N. JEFFERSON MILWAUKEE WI 53202

P: (414) 347-1100 F: (414) 347-1010

MARY PAT CUPERTINO
maryc@i777.com

INDEPENDENT

777 N. JEFFERSON   P: (414) 347-1100
MILW WI 53202   F: (414) 347-1010

INDEPENDENT

777 N. JEFFERSON MILW WI 53202   P: (414) 347-1100 F: (414) 347-1010

with compliments

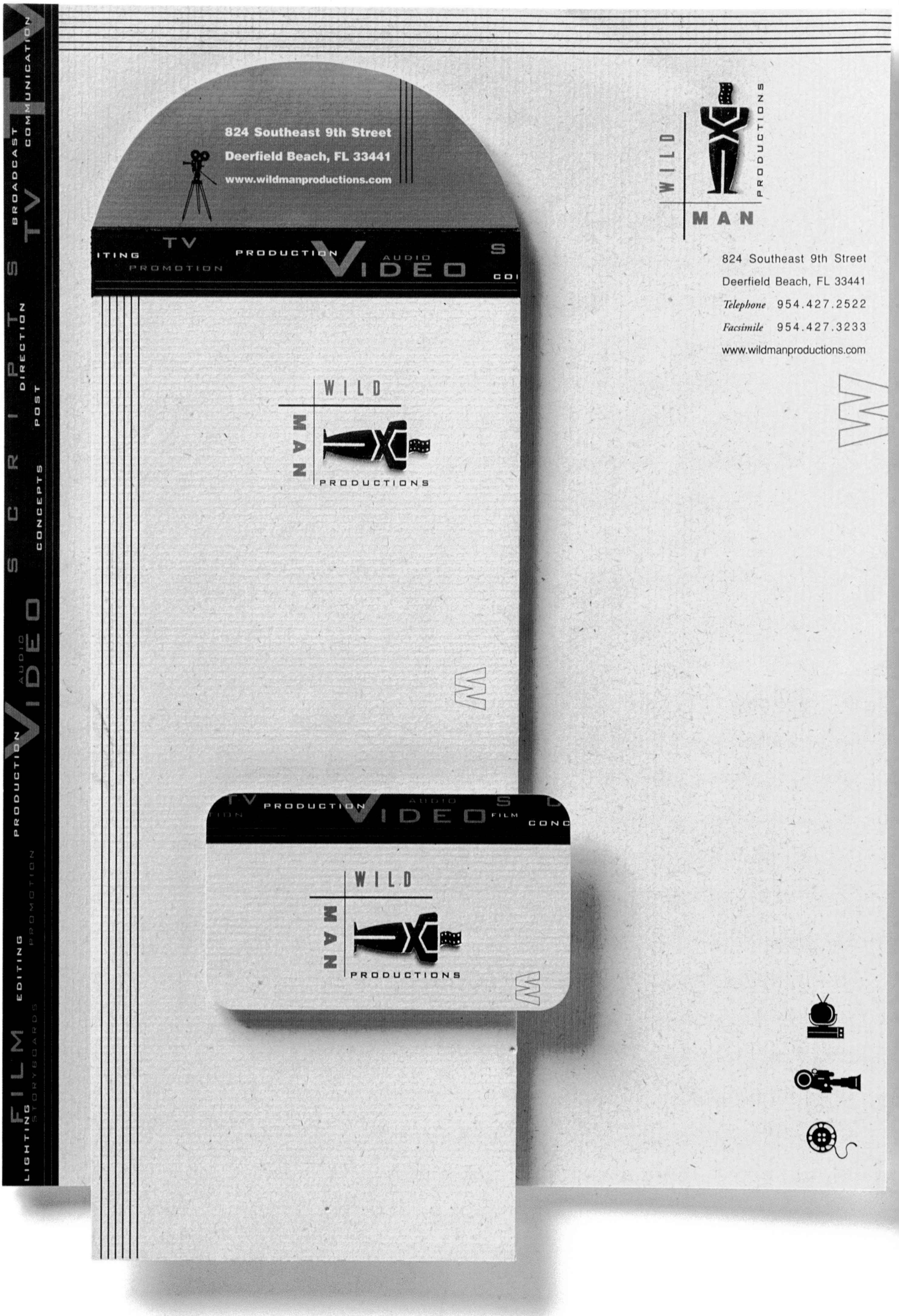

824 Southeast 9th Street
Deerfield Beach, FL 33441
www.wildmanproductions.com

WILD
MAN
PRODUCTIONS

824 Southeast 9th Street
Deerfield Beach, FL 33441
Telephone 954.427.2522
Facsimile 954.427.3233
www.wildmanproductions.com

San Francisco
Production Group

550 Bryant Street
San Francisco, CA 94107

San Francisco
Production Group

550 Bryant Street
San Francisco, CA 94107
phone: (415) 495.5595
fax: (415) 543.8370

Design Firm: **Morla Design** Art Director: **Jennifer Morla** Designers: **Jennifer Morla** and **Craig Bailey** Photographer: **Bettmann Archive** Client: **The Kobel Collection**

Film 106, 107

Design Firm: **Acorn Design Ltd.** Art Director: **Frank Chan** Designers: **Frank Chan** and **Louisa Law** Client: **Eulogia Productions Limited**

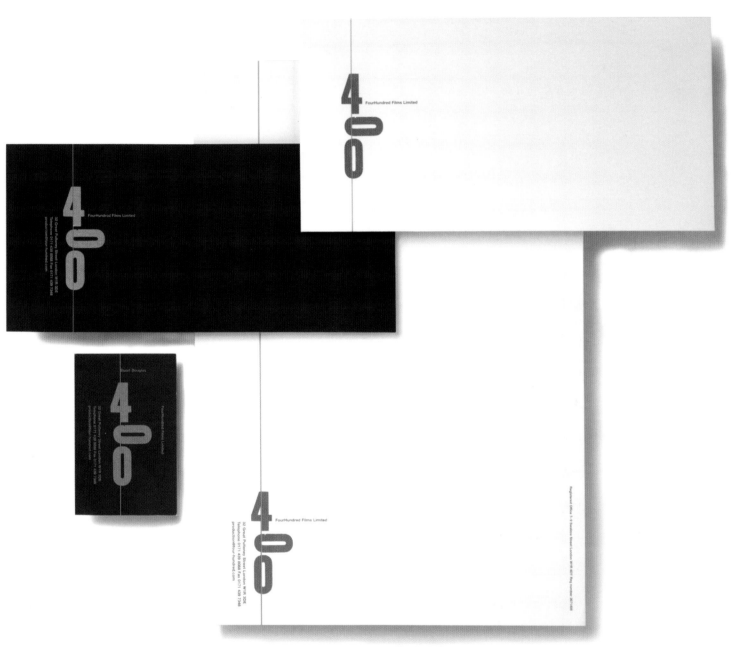

Design Firm: **Frost Design Ltd.** Art Director and Creative Director: **Vince Frost** Designers: **Vince Frost** and **Melanie Mules** Client: **400 Films Ltd.** Film 108, 109

GIL⁰VENTURES

P.O.BOX 620925
WOODSIDE, CALIFORNIA
94062.0925

WWW.GILOVENTURES.COM

PH (650)·851·5060
FX (650)·851·2887

P.O. BOX 620925
WOODSIDE, CA 94062.0925

◉ EMIKO HIGASHI   ◉ CEO
EMIKO@GILOVENTURES.COM

(OFFICES) · P.O.BOX 620925	4700 FALLS OF NEUSE RD., STE. 390	3 DANIEL FRISCH STREET	WWW.GILOVENTURES.COM
WOODSIDE, CALIFORNIA	RALEIGH, NORTH CAROLINA	TEL-AVIV, ISRAEL	
94062.0925	27609-6200	64731	

GIL⁰VENTURES

PH (650)·851·5060	PH (919)·713·4353	PH 972·3·6957740
FX (650)·851·2887	FX (919)·713·4336	FX 972·3·6957762

Design Firm: **I.M.S.** Art Director and Designer: **Jamie Anderson** Client: **Finatech Capital Group, Inc.**

Ambridge.

Ambridge
Investments Pty Ltd

Level 35, 140 William Street
Melbourne Victoria 3000
ACN 077 299 051

Telephone 61 3 9670 8877
Facsimile 61 3 9670 0511
admin@ambridge.com.au

Ambridge.

Ambridge Films Pty Ltd
Ambridge Investments Pty Ltd
Ambridge Finance Pty Ltd

Level 35, 140 William Street
Melbourne Victoria 3000
admin@ambridge.com.au

Telephone 61 3 9670 8877
Facsimile 61 3 9670 0511

Mark AC Stanley
Chief Executive Officer

Ambridge Investments Pty Ltd
Level 35, 140 William Street
Melbourne Victoria 3000
macs@ambridge.com.au

Telephone 61 3 9670 8877
Facsimile 61 3 9670 0511
Mobile 0411 864 444

Ambridge.

(s spread) Design Firm: **Fabio Ongarato Design** Art and Creative Director: **Fabio Ongarato** Designer: **Paul Tabouré** Client: **Ambridge Investments Pty Ltd.**

Ambridge have moved
into their new premises

Moved

Ambridge Investments Pty Ltd   Telephone 61 3 9670 8877
Level 35, 140 William Street   Facsimile 61 3 9670 0511
Melbourne Victoria 3000   admin@ambridge.com.au

Ambridge.

Design Firm: **Bianco & Cucco** Creative Directors: **Giovanni Bianco** and **Susanna Cucco** Designer: **Giovanni Bianco** Client: **Gentry Portorino**

Design Works Art Directors: Jack Anderson and Kathy Saito Designers: Kathy Saito, Sonia Max, Henry Yiu and Alan Copeland Client: InnoVentry

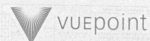

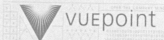

REMY VALENTE
OFFICE MANAGER

FOUR EXPRESSWAY PLAZA, 2ND FLOOR
ROSLYN HEIGHTS, NEW YORK 11577
T: 516-390-8800-x221 F: 516-390-8810
EMAIL: RVALENTE@VUEPOINT.COM
WWW.VUEPOINT.COM

YODLEE

595 LAWRENCE EXPRESSWAY
Sunnyvale, CA 94085

YODLEE

595 LAWRENCE EXPRESSWAY
Sunnyvale, CA 94085 USA

YODLEE

595 LAWRENCE EXPRESSWAY

YODLEE

Bank
Statements

Bills

Travel
Reservations

E-mail

Mobile/Wireless
Devices

YODLEE

595 LAWRENCE EXPRESSWAY
Sunnyvale, CA 94085 USA

DAVID DUNAWAY
Director, Business Development

www.yodlee.com

FIRST RESERVE™
BOTTLED IN U.S.A.
FLAGSTONE BREWERY
5916 AVELON VALLEY DRIVE NO.733
CHARLOTTE, N.C. 28277   54-22

FIRST RESERVE™
BOTTLED IN U.S.A.
FLAGSTONE BREWERY
5916 AVELON VALLEY DRIVE NO.733
CHARLOTTE, N.C. 28277

CHRIS WILLIAMS,
SPECIALTY BRAND DEVELOPMENT MANAGER

FIRST RESERVE™
BOTTLED IN U.S.A.
FLAGSTONE BREWERY
5916 AVELON VALLEY DRIVE NO.733
CHARLOTTE, N.C. 28277

PARCEL POST
CONTENTS: OFFICIAL

RETURN REQUESTED

FIRST RESERVE™
BOTTLED IN U.S.A.
FLAGSTONE BREWERY
5916 AVELON VALLEY DRIVE NO.733
CHARLOTTE, N.C. 28277

TO

54-22

TELEPHONE: (704) 341.9028
(770) 642.1246 – FAX: (704) 341.9029

Design Firm: **Templin Brink Design** Creative Directors: **Gaby Brink** and **Joel Templin** Designer: **Gaby Brink** Illustrator: **Elvis Swift** Client: **Kelham MacLean**

Food & Beverage 118,119

DELTA BEVERAGE GROUP

DELTA BEVERAGE GROUP

Liz Schaeffer
Brand Manager

2221 Democrat Road
Memphis, TN 38132
901-344-7100
901-344-7197 fax

DELTA BEVERAGE GROUP
1301 Aggie Road, Jonesboro, AR 72401

2221 Democrat Road, Memphis, TN 38132　●　901-344-7100 phone　901-344-7197 fax

The Food Bank

Keeping hunger at bay in Nebraska and western Iowa / Member of Second Harvest National Food Bank Network
6824 J St., Omaha, NE 68117-1016 / 402-331-1213 Fax: 402-331-6632 / www.discoveromaha.com/community/group/foodbank

The Food Bank

6824 J St., Omaha, NE 68117-1016
Phone: 402-331-1213
Fax: 402-331-6632

The Food Bank

6824 J St., Omaha, NE 68117-1016

Delicious Works of Art

MUSEUM
of Cakes

Delicious Works of Art

MUSEUM
of Cakes

Scott Snelgrove
1331 10th Street, NW • Washington, DC • 20001
P 202.903.8883 • F 202.518.9758
scott@museumofcakes.com
www.museumofcakes.com

Delicious Works of Art

MUSEUM
of Cakes

Scott Snelgrove • 1331 10th Street, NW • Washington, DC • 20001

1331 10th Street, NW • Washington, DC • 20001 • P 202.903.8883 • F 202.518.9758 • www.museumofcakes.com

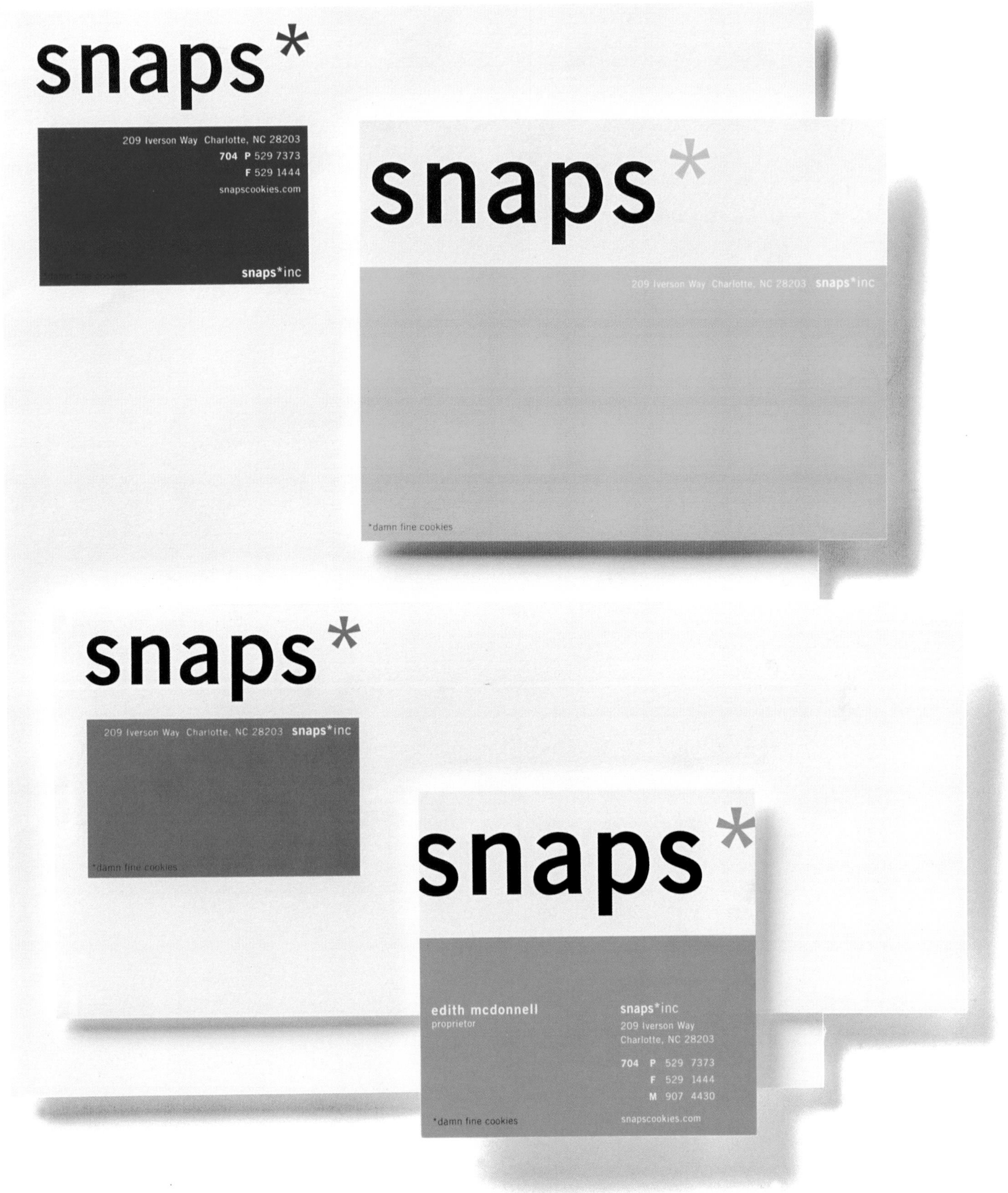

Design Firm: **Hawse Design, Inc.** Creative Director: **Robert Hawse** Designer, Copywriter and Illustrator: **Brady Bone** Client: **Snaps**

QZINA SPECIALTY FOODS INC.
110 WOODBINE DOWNS BLVD., #3
TORONTO, ONTARIO
CANADA M9W 5S6
T 416 675-2282
   888 816-6696
F 416 675-6255

QZINA SPECIALTY FOODS INC.
11851 HAMMERSMITH WAY
RICHMOND, BRITISH COLUMBIA
CANADA V7A 5E5
T 604 274-2626
   800 661-2462
F 604 274-2600

VANCOUVER   EDMONTON   TORONTO   SAN FRANCISCO   MIAMI

Design Firm: **Karacters Design Group** Art Director and Designer: **Michelle Metenchuk** Creative Director: **Maria Kennedy** Illustrator: **Ivan Angelic** Client: **Dynamic Chocolates**

SWEETISH HILL BAKERY 1120 West 6th St. Austin, TX 78703 Fax.472.6041 512.472.7370

SWEETISH HILL BAKERY 1120 West 6th St. Austin, TX 78703

SENOK™
TEA FOR THE SENSES

126 S Spokane Street | Seattle, WA 98124

SENOK™
TEA FOR THE SENSES

SENOK™
TEA FOR THE SENSES

Landy Pen

126 S Spokane Street | Seattle, WA 98124
P 206.903.0858 | 1.877.736.6583 | F 206.624.3026
lpen@senoktea.com | www.senoktea.com

126 S Spokane Street | Seattle, WA 98124
P 206.903.0858 | 1.877.736.6583 | F 206.624.3026
admin@senoktea.com | www.senoktea.com

126 S Spokane Street | Seattle, WA 98124

SENOK™
TEA FOR THE SENSES

Slow Cooked • *Easy to Prepare* • *Marinated* • *Great Tasting*

Post Office Box 2519
Wichita, Kansas 67201

PO Box 2519 Wichita, KS 672...

POST OFFICE BOX 15216   PORTLAND OREGON 97293   TELEPHONE 503 234 5261   CELLULAR 503 805 3422

Design Firm: **Lift Communications** Art Director, Creative Director and Designer: **Amy Devletian** Photographer: **Paul Foster** Client: **Half Moon Catering**

I N S I G H T

Insight Lighting Inc.

4341 Fulcrum Way NW

Rio Rancho, NM 87124

Tel: 505.345.0888

Fax: 505.345.3838

www.insightlighting.com

Insight Lighting Inc.

4341 Fulcrum Way NW

Rio Rancho, NM 87124

www.insightlighting.com

I N S I G H T

Insight Lighting Inc.

4341 Fulcrum Way NW

Rio Rancho, NM 87124

Tel: 505.345.0888

Fax: 505.345.3838

ramiro@insightlighting.com

I N S I G H T

Ramiro Barajas

Vice President Manufacturing/Engineering

I N S I G H T

Insight Lighting Inc.

4341 Fulcrum Way NW

Rio Rancho, NM 87124

SMILE

SMILE

8410-A FALLS OF NEUSE ROAD RALEIGH NC 27615

Dr. Gregg Michael Festa DDS
8410-A FALLS OF NEUSE ROAD RALEIGH NC 27615 919.847.3899

P A N O R A M A   D E N T A L   G R O U P

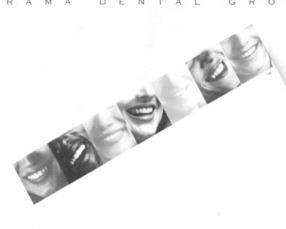

P A N O R A M A   D E N T A L   G R O U P ™

CHRISTOPHER J. HEINY, D.D.S.

THE CENTER FOR COSMETIC & RESTORATIVE DENTISTRY
9025 E. MINERAL CIRCLE #200, ENGLEWOOD, CO 80112
TELEPHONE: (303) 790-2273 FAX: (303) 790-2973

THE CENTER FOR COSMETIC & RESTORATIVE DENTISTRY
9025 E. MINERAL CIRCLE #200, ENGLEWOOD, CO 80112
TELEPHONE: (303) 790-2273 FAX: (303) 790-2973

1003 DIAMOND AVE. • STE. 200 • SO. PASADENA CA • 91030

1003 DIAMOND AVE. • STE. 200 • SO. PASADENA, CA. • 91030

SEND TO

DAVID TILLINGHAST

DAVID TILLINGHAST

1003 DIAMOND AVE. • STE. 200 • SO. PASADENA CA • 91030
818·403·0991 PHONE
818·403·0993 FAX
DAVID TILLINGHAST

DAVID TILLINGHAST

1003 DIAMOND AVE. • STE. 200 • S.O. PASADENA, CA. • 91030

Design Firm: **Arkkit-Forms Design** Art Directors and Designers: **David McCarski** and **Kymberly Jefferies** Illustrator: **David Tillinghast** Client: **David Tillinghast** Health, Illustrations 136,137

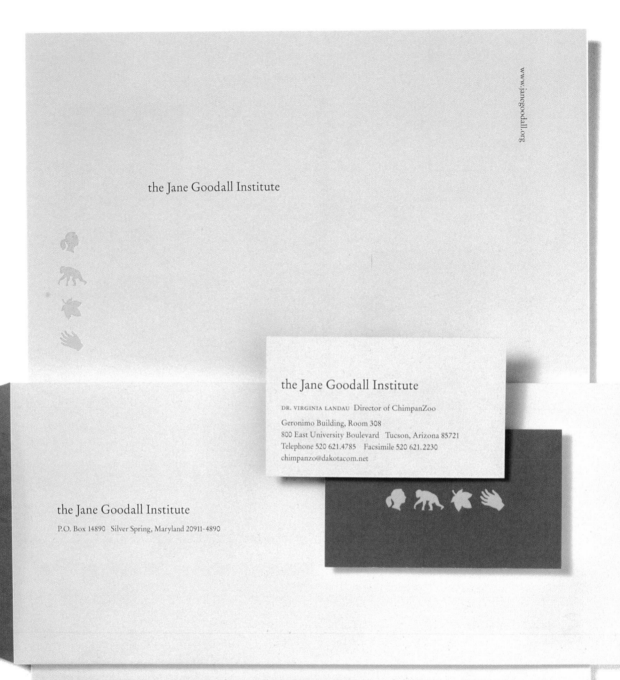

the Jane Goodall Institute

www.janegoodall.org

the Jane Goodall Institute

DR. VIRGINIA LANDAU Director of ChimpanZoo

Geronimo Building, Room 308
800 East University Boulevard   Tucson, Arizona 85721
Telephone 520 621.4785   Facsimile 520 621.2230
chimpanzo@dakotacom.net

the Jane Goodall Institute

P.O. Box 14890 Silver Spring, Maryland 20911-4890

P.O. Box 14890 Silver Spring, Maryland 20911-4890   Telephone 301 565.0086   Facsimile 301 565.3188

mixed greens

601 WEST 26TH STREET | 11TH FLOOR | NEW YORK | NY | 10001
T: 212 331 8868 | F: 212 343 2134

LAYLA LOZANO

mixed greens

601 WEST 26TH STREET | 11TH FLOOR | NEW YORK | NY | 10001
T: 212 331 8868 | F: 212 343 2134 | LAYLA@MIXEDGREENS.COM

WWW.MIXEDGREENS.COM

KELLY STOETZEL

mixed greens

601 WEST 26TH STREET | 11TH FLOOR | NEW YORK | NY | 10001
T: 212 331 8868 | F: 212 343 2134 | KELLY@MIXEDGREENS.COM

ANNE-MARIE BUSDELL

mixed greens

601 WEST 26TH STREET | 11TH FLOOR | NEW YORK | NY | 10001
T: 212 331 8868 | F: 212 343 2134 | ANNE@MIXEDGREENS.COM

WWW.MIXEDGREENS.COM

PAIGE WEST

mixed greens

601 WEST 26TH STREET | 11TH FLOOR | NEW YORK | NY | 10001
T: 212 331 8868 | F: 212 343 2134 | PAIGE@MIXEDGREENS.COM

AMAZON.COM

1516 SECOND AVENUE | SEATTLE, WASHINGTON 98101 | TEL 206-622-2335 | FAX 206-622-2405

JEFF BEZOS
FOUNDER, PRESIDENT, CEO

AMAZON.COM

1516 SECOND AVENUE | SEATTLE, WASHINGTON 98101
TEL 206-622-2335 | FAX 206-622-2405
E-MAIL JEFFBEZOS@AMAZON.COM

130 West 17th Street
Second Floor
New York, NY 10011

Telephone 212.604.0900
          800.257.7764
Facsimile 212.414.2753
mail @ realfurniture.com

REALfurniture com

Mark Logan
Jack of All Trades

130 West 17th Street 2nd Floor
New York, NY 10011

Telephone 212.604.0900
          800.257.7764
Facsimile 212.414.2753
Cellular   203.984.0484

mark @ realfurniture.com

REALfurniture com

M. Sammye Akutsu
Chief Cook & Bottle Washer

130 West 17th Street 2nd Floor
New York, NY 10011

Telephone 212.604.0900
          800.257.7764
Facsimile 212.414.2753
Cellular   617.448.4275

sammye @ realfurniture.com

REALfurniture com

Claudia Carmel
Sleuth

130 West 17th Street 2nd Floor
New York, NY 10011

Telephone 212.604.0900
          800.257.7764
Facsimile 212.414.2753

claudia @ realfurniture.com

REALfurniture com

Abby Suckle. AIA
Major Domo

130 West 17th Street 2nd Floor
New York, NY 10011

Telephone 212.604.0900
          800.257.7764
Facsimile 212.414.2753
Cellular   917.686.3229

abby @ realfurniture.com

REALfurniture com

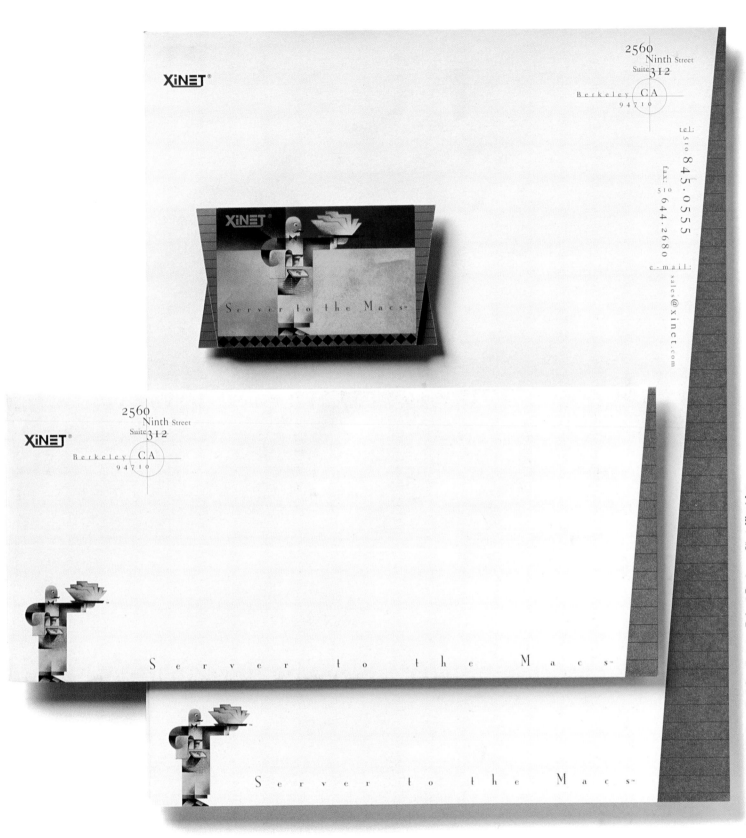

Design Firm: **Gee & Chung Design** Art Director, Creative Director and Designer: **Earl Gee** Illustrator: **Robert Pastrana** Client: **Xinet Inc.**

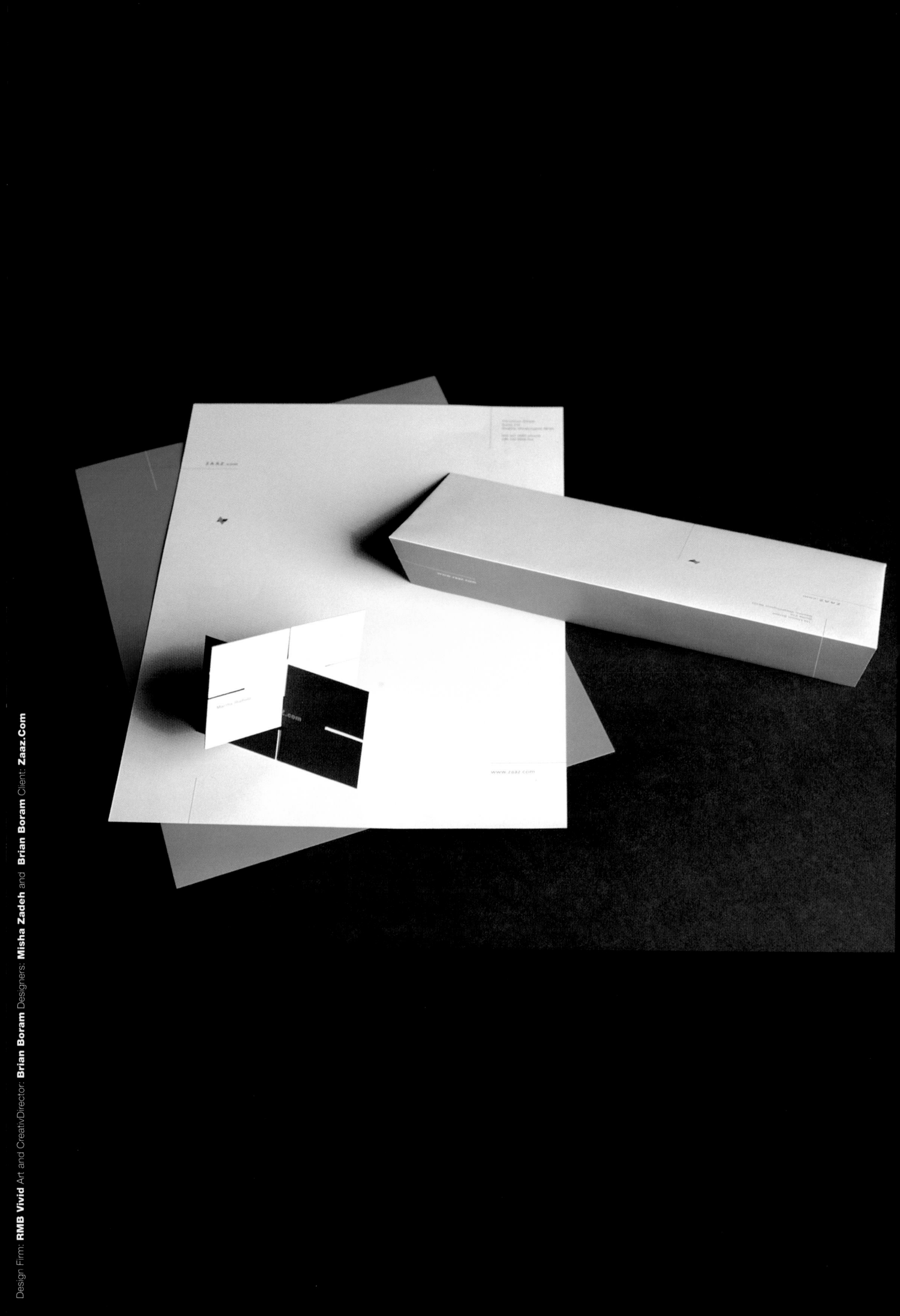

Design Firm: **RMB Vivid** Art and CreativDirector: **Brian Boram** Designers: **Misha Zadeh** and **Brian Boram** Client: **Zaaz.Com**

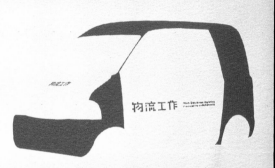

Packaging Create Inc. Art Director: **Akio Okumura** Designer: **Yasuyo Fukumoto** Client: **Japan Bridge**

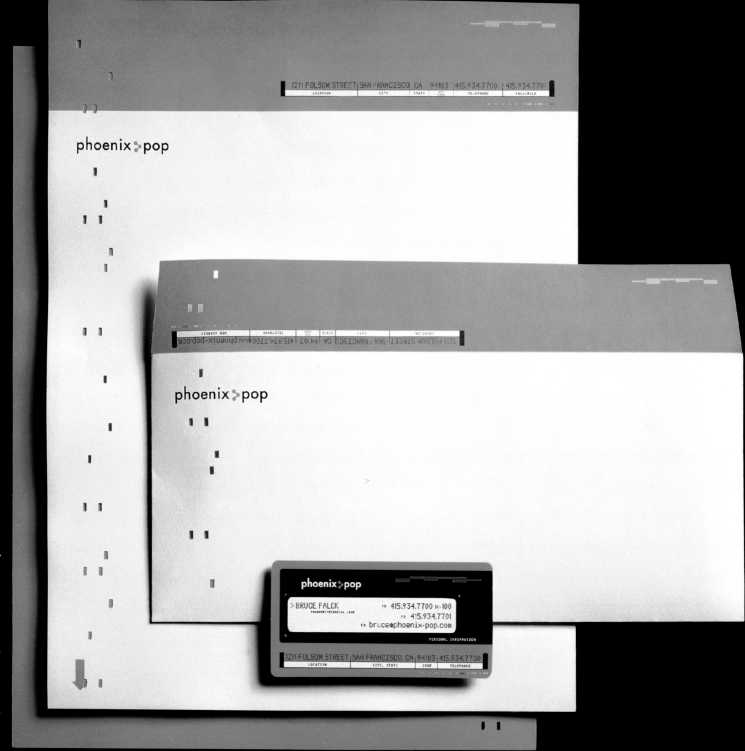

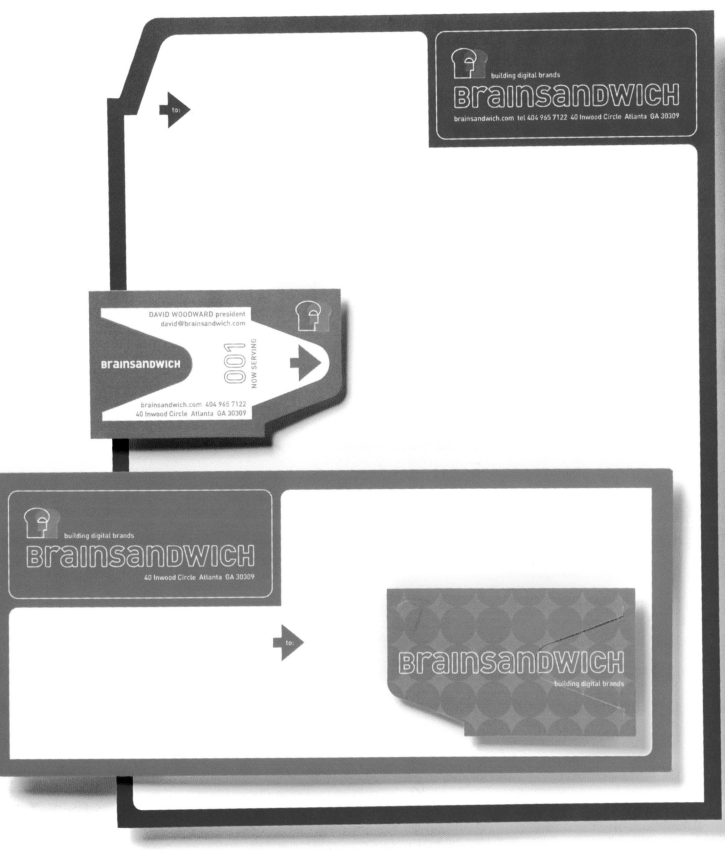

Design Firm: **Iconologic** Creative Director: **Brad Copeland** Designer and Illustrator: **Lea Nihcols Friedman** Client: **Brainsandwich**

Michael J. Berent
michael.berent@marchfirst.com

320 N. Elizabeth Street
Chicago, IL 60607
312 913 3377 tel
312 913 6967 fax
www.marchfirst.com

MUSEUM OF COLLECTIBLE ARTS ONLINE
1523 P ST, NW, WASHINGTON, DC 20005
TEL: 202.667.1752 FAX: 202.234.1466
E-MAIL: MOCASHOP@AOL.COM
WWW.MOCAONLINE.COM

M O
C A
ONLINE.COM

MUSEUM OF COLLECTIBLE ARTS ONLINE
114 BRADLEY CREEK CROSSING
SAVANNAH, GEORGIA 31410
TEL: 912.897.1540 FAX: 912.897.1543
E-MAIL: KGUEST@EMAIL.MSN.COM
WWW.MOCAONLINE.COM

Katherine Guest

M O
C A
ONLINE.COM

MUSEUM OF COLLECTIBLE ARTS ONLINE
1523 P ST, NW, WASHINGTON, DC 20005

M O
C A
ONLINE.COM

britart.com

britart.com

67 Roman Road Bethnal Green London E2 0QN   t 020 8980 7272   f 020 8980 7373   e info@britart.com
company reg. no.3883334 vat reg. no.749 7107 03

britart.com

richard murphy
marketing director

67 Roman Road Bethnal Green London E2 0QN
t 020 8980 7272 f 020 8980 7373 m 0780 1236325
e richard@britart.com

67 Roman Road Bethnal Green London E2 0QN   t 020 8980 7272   f 020 8980 7373   e info@britart.com
company reg. no.3883334 vat reg. no.749 7107 03

Design Firm: **Mother Ltd.** Art Directors and Designers: **Markus Bjurman, Cecelia Dafils** and **Kim Lehrig** Creative Director: **Mark Waites** Copywriters: **Jo de Souza, Markus Bjurman, Cecelia Dufils** and **Kim Lehrig** Client: **Britart.com**   Internet 150,151

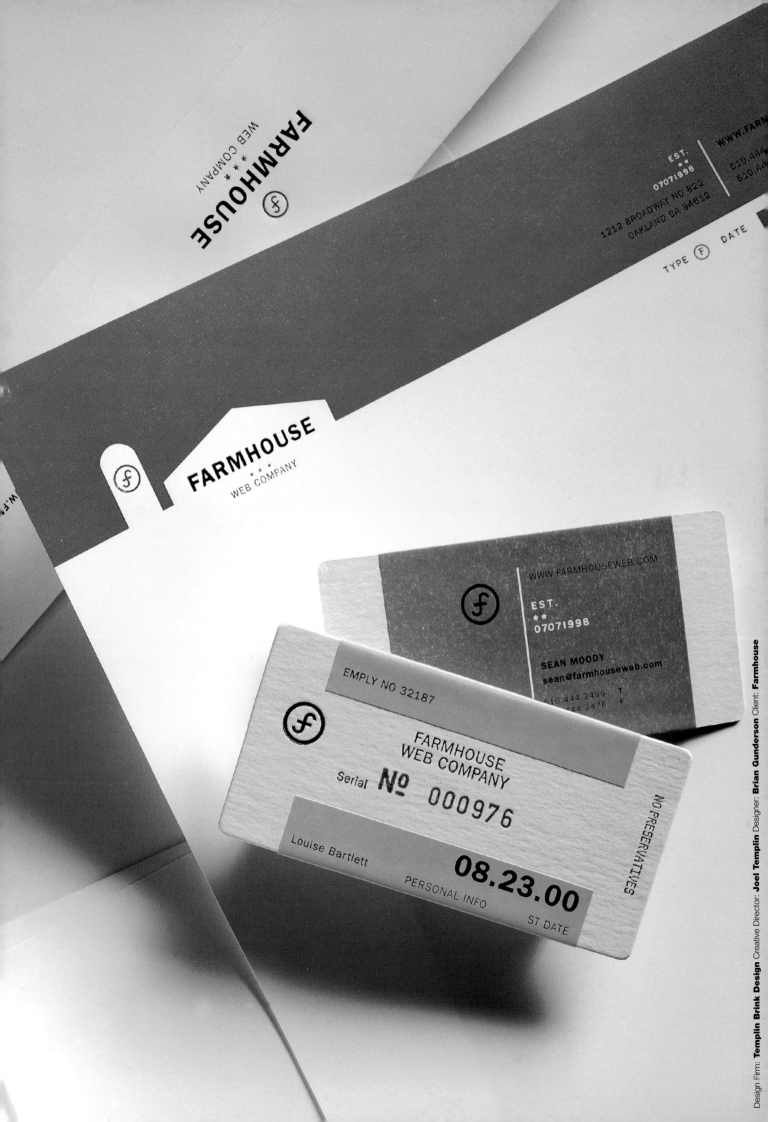

sven fuchs <anwendungs_entwicklung>

internett gmbh
richard-wagner-str. 14-16
(haus der zukunft)
66111 saarbrücken

telefon (0681) 950 95-0
direkt (0681) 950 95-16
telefax (0681) 950 95-99

http://internett.de
s.fuchs@internett.de

internett gmbh
> gesellschaft für informations- und kommunikationstechnik

internett gmbh > gesellschaft für informations- und kommunikationstechnik

> richard-wagner-str. 14-16 (haus der zukunft) > 66111 saarbrücken
> telefon: (0681) 950 95 - 0 > telefax: (0681) 950 95 - 99
> http://www.internett.de/ > kontakt@internett.de

amtsgericht saarbrücken hrb 11427
> geschäftsführer: hendrik becker
> bankverbindung: sparkasse saarbrücken
blz 590 501 01 > konto 900 16 536

internett gmbh

> gesellschaft für informations- und kommunikationstechnik > richard-wagner-str. 14-16 (haus der zukunft) > 66111 saarbrücken

1016 1st Avenue, 4th Floor
Seattle, Washington 98104
T 206.223.0390
F 206.749.0378
M 206.669.2768
jason@punkt.ws
www.punkt.ws

jason thomas faulkner

brand x
1415 western avenue, suite 600, seattle, wa 98101
www.brandx.com

>>> AN INTERNET MARKETING COMPANY <<<

JOHN IRWIN
general manager
tel 206 361 9990
ext 112
john@brandx.com

brand x
1415 western avenue, suite 600, seattle, wa 98101
www.brandx.com

>>> AN INTERNET MARKETING COMPANY   >>> VISIT US AT: WWW.BRANDX.COM

brand x   1415 western avenue, suite 600, seattle, wa 98101
www.brandx.com

Design Firm: **PunktArt** Director, Designer and Illustrator: **Jason Thomas Faulkner** Copywriter: **Jason Thomas Faulkner** Client: **Brand X**   Internet 154, 155

2483 E. Bayshore Rd.
Suite 202
Palo Alto CA 94303

650 320 2222 main
650 320 2223 fax
www.zadu.com

zadu™

Ovanes Markarian
Developer

zadu

Plinganserstrasse 8
D-81369 München
(089) 729 499 52 tel
(089) 767 032 40 fax
omarkarian@zadu.com

Christian Wiener
Creative Director and
Co-Founder

zadu

Plinganserstrasse 8
D-81369 München
(089) 729 499 52 tel
(089) 767 032 40 fax
cwiener@zadu.com

2483 E. Bayshore Rd.
Suite 202
Palo Alto CA 94303

zadu™

novo interactive

novo interactive

222 Sutter Street, Sixth Floor San Francisco, California 94108

Digital Commerce Architects

novo interactive

222 Sutter Street, Sixth Floor San Francisco, California 94108 t **415 646 7000** f 415 646 7001 www.novointeractive.com

Design Firm: **Templin Brink Design** Creative Director and Designer: **Joel Templin** Client: **Sparks.com**

Design Firm: **Hornall Anderson Design Works Inc.** Art Director: **Lisa Cerveny** Designers: **Lisa Cerveny, Michael Brugman** and **Mary Hermes** Client: **Hardware.com**

gettuit.com

Natacha Gaymer-Jones
Multimedia Services
Specialist

4010 Lake Washington
Boulevard N.E.
Suite 300

Kirkland
Washington
98033-7866

tel. 425.739.9811
fax 425.828.2580

natacha@gettuit.com

gettuit.com

gettuit.com

gettuit.com

4010 Lake Washington
Boulevard N.E
Suite 300

Kirkland
Washington

98033-7866

Design Firm: **Hornall Anderson Design Works Inc.** Art Director: **Jack Anderson** Designers: **Kathy Saito, Gretchen Cook, James Tee, Julie Lock, Henry Yiu, Alan Copeland** and **Sonja Max** Client: **Gettuit.**

Hornall Anderson Design Works Inc. Art Director: **Katha Dalton** Designers: **Katha Dalton, Bruce Benson-Meyer, Michael Brugman, Mary Hermes, Tobi Brown** and **Ed Lee** Client: **Aptimus**

ofoto

ofoto, inc.
1802 fifth street
berkeley ca 94710

www.ofoto.com

tel 510 649 4700
fax 510 649 4706

ofoto

adam policky
graphic designer

adam@ofoto.com
tel 510 647 0513
fax 510 649 4706

ofoto, inc.
1802 fifth street
berkeley ca 94710

www.ofoto.com

ofoto

ofoto, inc.
1802 fifth street
berkeley ca 94710

www.ofoto.com

Design Firm: **The Salamander** Creative Director and Designer: **Gregoire Vion Client: Ofoto**

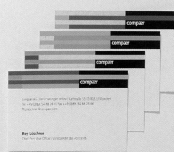

freestyle
interactive

freestyle
interactive
58 Second Street, San Francisco, California 94105 www.freestyleinteractive.com

freestyle
interactive

58 Second Street, San Francisco, California 94105
t 415 778 0610 f 415 778 0614
www.freestyleinteractive.com

58 Second Street, San Francisco, California 94105
t 415 778 0610 f 415 778 0614
www.freestyleinteractive.com

Design Firm: **Oh Boy, A Design Company** Creative Director: **David Salanitro** Designer: **Hunter Wimmer** Client: **Freestyle Interactive**

∫

S U M E N T O L A & I T Ä L Ä

∫

S U M E N T O L A & I T Ä L Ä

SAATE

O SOPIMUKSEN MUKAAN

O TOIMENPITEITÄNNE VARTEN

O ASIAKIRJAT PYYDETÄÄN PALAUTTAMAAN

O PUHELINKESKUSTELUUN VIITATEN

O TIEDOKSI

O PALAUTETAAN

O ALLEKIRJOITETTAVAKSI

O PYYDETÄÄN ANTAMAAN TIEDOKSI

ASIANAJOTOIMISTO SUMENTOLA & ITÄLÄ OY
ATTORNEYS AT LAW | LAWYERS
Kauppiaskatu 5 20100 Turku Finland
TEL:+358 2 273 0200 FAX:+358 2 251 3913
EMAIL: office@sumentola-itala.fi
WEBSITE: www.sumentola-itala.fi
TR.REG. NO: 609.533

S U M E N T O L A & I T Ä L Ä

Design Firm: **Heye & Partner** Art Director and Designer: **Alexander Emil Möller** Client: **Su Bühler**

ESPECIALLY PREPARED FOR:

DELEO CLAY
TILE COMPANY
MANUFACTURERS OF
THROUGHBODY TILES

600 Chaney Street
Lake Elsinore
California 92530
Tel 909 674 1578
Pgr 909 672 5945
Fax 909 245 2427
www.deleoclaytile.com

STEVE BRUNELLE
Sales and Architectural Rep.

YOUR VISION IN TILE.

Welcome to the world of Deleo Clay Tile. Whether you're looking
for a custom hue, or specific shapes to
complement a wide array of building styles, you can find
them all here. Deleo Clay Tile. Where
nature's finest roofing material achieves its fullest potential.

MADE IN AMERICA

DELEO CLAY
MANUFACTURERS
600 Chaney Stre
Lake Elsinore, Ca
Tel 909 674 1578
Fax 909 245 2427
www.deleoclaytile.com

DELEO CLAY TILE COMPANY
MANUFACTURERS OF THROUGHBODY TILES

600 Chaney Street
Lake Elsinore, California 92530
Tel 909 674 1578   800 654 1119
Fax 909 245 2427
www.deleoclaytile.com

YOUR VISION IN TILE

THANK YOU

MANUFACTURERS OF QUALITY

Trade   Mark

DELEO CLAY TILE CO.

MADE IN THE USA
EST. 1984

THROUGHBODY CLAY TILES

600 Chaney Street Lake Elsinore, California 92530 www.deleoclaytile.com

Dr. med. Hilmar Fleischer
Chirurg

78647 Trossingen
Schlehdornweg 2
Telefon: 07425-4024

Dr. med. Hilmar Fleischer
Chirurg

78647 Trossingen
Schlehdornweg 2
Telefon: 07425-4024

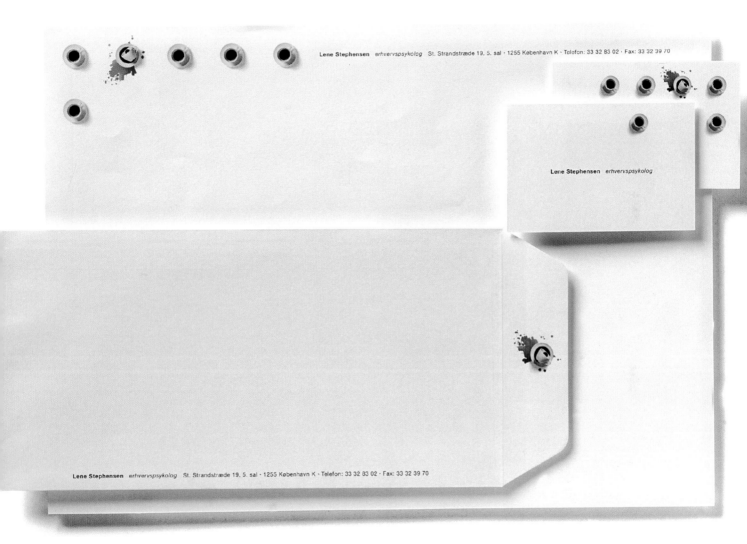

Design Firm: **BBDO A/S** Art Director and Designer: **Lars Hartmann** Photographer: **Jacob Gils** Client: **Lene Stephensen**

Medicine 172,173

Dorn im Auge

Dorn im Auge

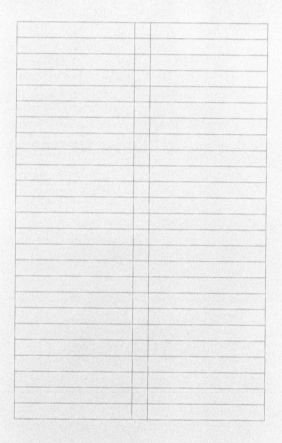

Dorn im Auge

Charles Greene
Geschäftsführer

Dorn im Auge GmbH • Werbeagentur
Königsberger Straße 1 • 40231 Düsseldorf
e-mail charles@dorn-im-auge.com
Fon (0211) 97 38-212 • Fax (0211) 97 38-201
Mobil (0177) 8 44 44 66

Dorn im Auge GmbH • Werbeagentur • Königsberger Straße 1
40231 Düsseldorf • Telefon + 49 (211) 97 38 212 • Telefax + 49 (211) 97 38 201
Mobil (01 77) 8 44 44 66 • charles@dorn-im-auge.com

Dorn im Auge GmbH • Werbeagentur • Königsberger Straße 1 • 40231 Düsseldorf • Fon (0211) 97 38-212 • Fax (0211) 97 38-201
Mobil (01 77) 8 44 44 66 • charles@dorn-im-auge.com • Geschäftsführer: Charles Greene • Amtsgericht Düsseldorf • HRB 39143
Dresdner Bank Düsseldorf • BLZ 300 800 00 • Konto 211 006 400

the Dental Center
of Stamford

the Dental Center
587 Elm Street
Stamford, CT 06902

t: (203) 969-0802
f: (203) 326-2990

the Dental Center
of Stamford

the Dental Center
587 Elm Street
Stamford, CT 06902

t: (203) 969-0802
f: (203) 326-2990

Linda J. Ferraro, RDH
Clinic Coordinator

Design Firm: **Taylor Design** Art Director: **Daniel Taylor** Designer: **Mark Barrett** Client: **The Dental Center**

THE SKYSCRAPER MUSEUM
44 WALL STREET, NY NY 10005
OFFICE: 5 E 22 ST. 30 F, NY, NY 10010
TELEPHONE: 212-968-1961
FACSIMILE: 212-677-7325

CAROL WILLIS, DIRECTOR

THE SKYSCRAPER MUSEUM
44 WALL STREET, NY NY 10005
OFFICE: 5 E 22 ST. 30 F, NY, NY 10010
TELEPHONE: 212-968-1961
FACSIMILE: 212-677-7325

THE SKYSCRAPER MUSEUM
44 WALL STREET, NY NY 10005
OFFICE: 5 E 22 ST. 30 F, NY, NY 10010

One Complimentary Guest Pass to

"Canada's Flying Museum"

Open
daily

Don Murray
Building Services

Tel 905 679-4183 X 224
Fax 905 679-4186

CANADIAN
WARPLANE
HERITAGE
MUSEUM

9280 Airport Rd., Mt. Hope, ON Canada L0R 1W0
E-mail: museum@warplane.com Web: www.warplane.com

CANADIAN
WARPLANE
HERITAGE
MUSEUM

9280 Airport Rd., Mt. Hope, ON Canada L0R 1W0 Tel 905 679-4183 Fax 905 679-4186 E-mail: museum@warplane.com Web: www.warplane.com

Patron, His Royal Highness The Prince of Wales
Canadian Warplane Heritage is a federally registered Canadian Charity

CANADIAN
WARPLANE
HERITAGE
MUSEUM

Hamilton Airport, 9280 Airport Rd., Mt. Hope, ON Canada L0R 1W0

AMERICAN
MUSEUM
OF MINIATURE ARTS

AMERICAN
MUSEUM
OF MINIATURE ARTS

Janet L. Wilhite
Executive Director

2001 North Lamar Street
Dallas, Texas 75202
Tel 214.969.5502
Fax 214.969.5997

minimuseum@aol.com

Executive Director
Janet Wilhite

Honorary Committee
Walter & Pat Arnell
Dick & Mary Anne Cree
Nancy Hamon
Edmund Hoffman
S. Roger Horchow
Dan & Billie Krausse
Barbara Thomas Lemmon
Irvin Levy
Margaret Lowdon
Stanley Marcus
Harold Simmons
Jere Thompson
Otto K. Wetzell
Charles Wyly

Advisory Committee
Dorothy Harrison
Gay Hendrix
Margaret Lowdon
E.G. (Bud) Mantz

AMERICAN
MUSEUM
OF MINIATURE ARTS

2001 North Lamar Street   Dallas, Texas 75202   Tel 214.969.5502   Fax 214.969.5997   E-mail minimuseum@aol.com

Design Firm: **Sullivan Perkins** Art Director and Designer: **Myra J. Nowlin** Client: **American Museum of Miniature Arts**

Toledo Museum of Art

P.O. Box 1013, Toledo, Ohio 43697

Toledo Museum of Art

Rochelle R. Slosser
Graphic Design
Coordinator

Toledo Museum of Art
P.O. Box 1013
Toledo, Ohio 43697
419.254.5079
419.255.8000 ext. 7255
419.255.8551 fax
rslosser@toledomuseum.org

RACHEL SMY

HONEY MUSIC LTD
THE HEAL'S BUILDING ALFRED MEWS LONDON W1P 9LB TELEPHONE 020 7323 6755

HONEY MUSIC LTD THE HEAL'S BUILDING ALFRED MEWS LONDON W1P 9LB TELEPHONE 020 7323 6755

HONEY MUSIC LTD 122 BELLENDEN ROAD LONDON SE15 4RF TELEPHONE 020 7732 5312
VAT REGISTERED No.7222B0266 REGISTERED No.3631185 REGISTERED OFFICE 25 VILLIERS STREET LONDON WC2N 6ND

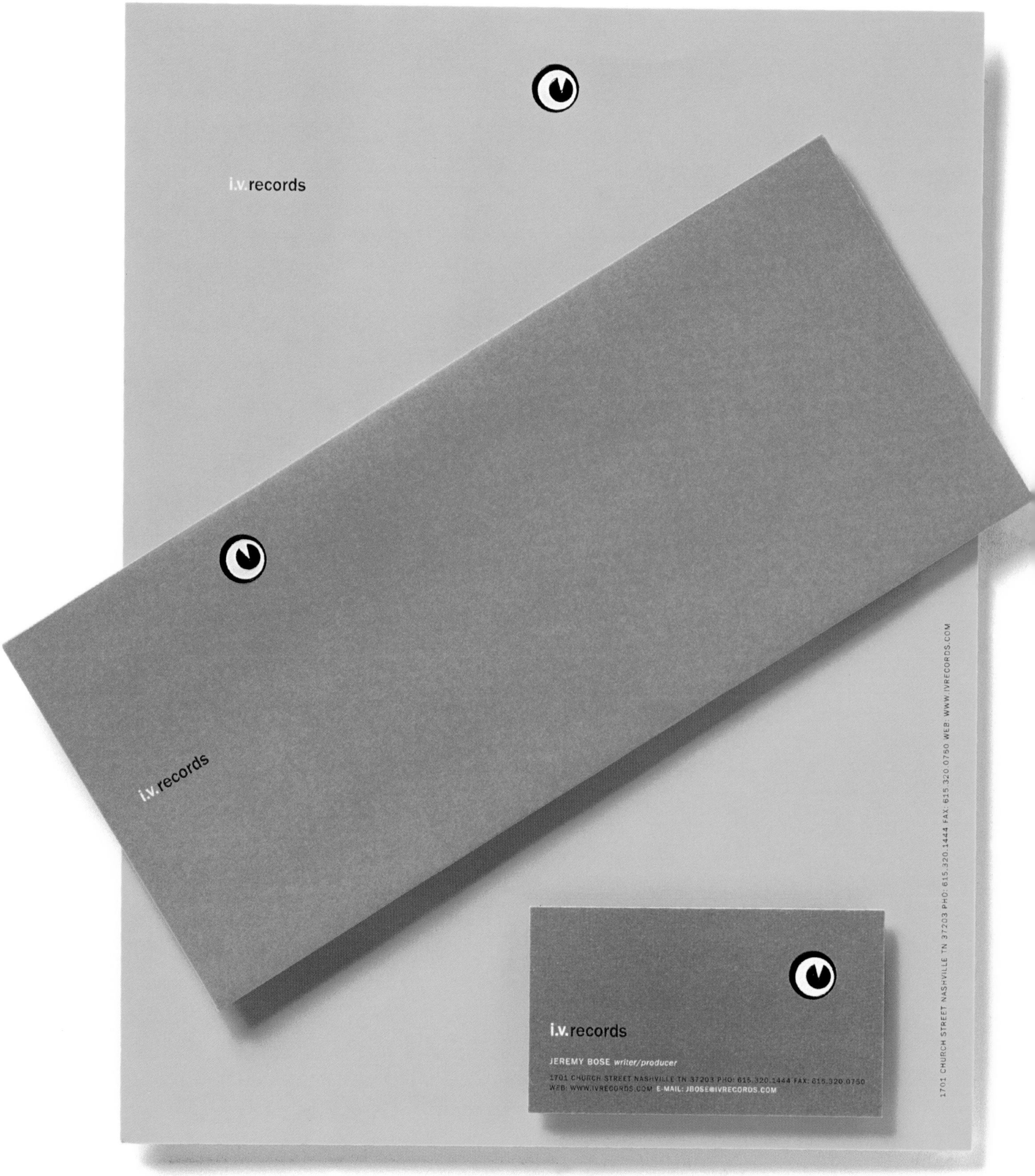

Design Firm: **Lewis Communications/Nashville** Art Director, Designer and Copywriter: **Robert Froedge** Client: **I.V. Records**

Random Bus

Date

305 East 46th Street, Beautiful New York City
New York, 10017-3058 United States of America
Telephone 212 980 0300 Facsimile 212 755 1737

TO

Random Bus

305 East 46th Street, Beautiful New York City
New York, 10017-3058 United States of America
Telephone 212 980 0300 Facsimile 212 755 1737

TO

Random Bus

Design Firm: **Sagmeister Inc.** Art Director: **Stefan Sagmeister** Designer: **Eric Zim** Photographer: **Tom Schierlitz** Client: **Random Bus**

NAKED MUSIC NYC

270 Lafayette Street Suite 904 New York NY 10012
Telephone 212 431 6745 Facsimile 212 431 6583

NAKED MUSIC NYC

Jay Denes

T. 212 431 6745 F. 431 6583
270 Lafayette Street #904
New York NY 10012

Naked Music NYC   270 Lafayette Street Suite 904 New York New York 10012 United States of America   **NAKED MUSIC NYC**

NEW LEAF
PAPER

NEW LEAF
PAPER

JEFF MENDELSOHN
President

TEL 415.291.9210
T.888.989.5323
215 Leidesdorff St. 4th floor
San Francisco, CA 94111

FAX 415.291.9353
jeff@newleafpaper.com
www.newleafpaper.com

NEW LEAF
PAPER

215 Leidesdorff St. 4th floor
San Francisco, CA 94111

215 Leidesdorff St. 4th floor SAN FRANCISCO CA 94111   EMAIL info@newleafpaper.com   185 Varick Street, 5th floor NEW YORK NY 10014
TEL 415.291.9210 FAX 415.291.9353   www.newleafpaper.com   TEL 212.645.5252 FAX 212.645.2304

SM**A**RT

THINKER

SM**A**RT

LETTER

SM**A**RT

PROFILES

SM**A**RT

WHEN I WANT TO BE

SM**A**RT

SOLUTIONS

SM**A**RT

SAMPLES

SM**A**RT

MAIL

SMART PAPERS
VERSATILITY, CHOICE AND PERFORMANCE

SMART PAPERS
VERSATILITY, CHOICE AND PERFORMANCE

INTERNATIONAL PAPER

SMART PAPERS
VERSATILITY, CHOICE AND PERFORMANCE

800.443.9773
WWW.SMARTPAPERS.COM

curious paper collection

curious paper collection | **Popset** has a unique pearlescent finish that brings a new and unexpected dimension to graphic design: the colors on these optical-effect papers actually "flip" (and you will, too!) under shifting light. | **Keaykolour Metallics** have a surface sheen evocative of sheared metal, creating a glittering play of light in a range of alloy hues while delivering superb printability – and passing effortlessly through airport security. | **Canson Satin** established the worldwide quality benchmark for translucent papers, then raised that mark higher with an unrivaled selection of exciting designer colors. | **LightSpeck** is the original white-flecked paper, a superior-quality recycled sheet with pale fibers...speckles...sprinkles...anyway, little bits of something lighter than the rest of the paper, including flecks of gold and silver. | **Conqueror** is an internationally available cotton-content letterhead range, competitively priced for the U.S. and featuring a localized watermark for great stationery design, plus specialty finishes such as ultra-smooth CX22. | **Sensation** is a revolutionary feltmarked sheet that brings unparalleled high-quality reproduction of full-color imagery to the world of uncoated papers. Arjo Wiggins Fine Papers | c/o 825 East Wisconsin Avenue | Appleton | WI 54911 | USA | **T** 920.830.4010 | **F** 920.830.4016 | Toll-free 1.800.779.0872 | www.curiouspapers.com

curious paper collection

Sarah Desmond | Sales & Marketing Coordinator
Arjo Wiggins Fine Papers | c/o 825 East Wisconsin Avenue | Appleton | WI 54911 | USA
T 920.830.4010 | **F** 920.830.4016 | **Direct** 1.800.779.0872 | sarah@curiouspapers.com
www.curiouspapers.com

curious paper collection

Design Firm: **Viva Dolan Communications & Design Inc.** Art Director: **Frank Viva** Designer: **Dominic Ayre** Copywriter: **Doug Dolan** Client: **Curious Paper (Arjo Wiggins Fine Paper)**

Wartburgstr. 48
D-10823 Berlin
T (+30) 781 93 74
(0172) 316 70 80
jaques@berlin.snafu.de
bagios@lbwel.com

BAGIOS
aka JAQUES BAGIOS

Est. 1968

2103 BONGEY DRIVE ◆ MENOMONIE, WI 54751

2103 BONGEY DRIVE ◆ MENOMONIE, WI 54751

Design Firm: **DBD International Ltd.** Art Director, Creative Director, Designer and Illustrator: **David Brier** Client: **David and Sherry Brier**

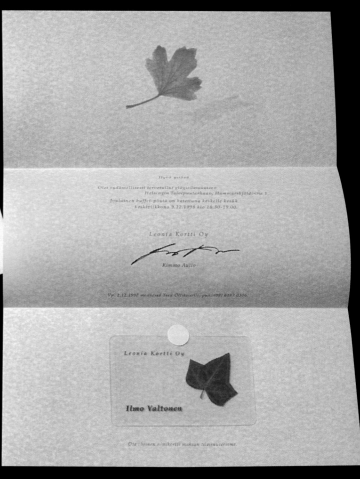

5-3-6 Akasaka
Minato-ku Tokyo 107-8006
Tel. 03-3746-1111

Design Firm: **E Co., Ltd.** Art Director: **Tatsuo Ebina** Creative Director: **Masaru Kitakaze** Designer: **Shigeyuki Ohgi** Copywriter: **Hideki Azuma** Client: **TBS Radio & Communications**   Personal 190,191

AJAY SALVI 556 JASDANWALA COMPOUND ALCO COMPANY
GODOWN N.M.JOSHI MARG BYCULLA (WEST)
MUMBAI 400 011 TEL 309 4385 FAX 309 4769 M 98200 35 120
Email ajaysalvi@vsnl.com website www.ajaysalvi.com

Design Firm: **Clockwork Apple Inc.** Designer and Photographer: **Christo Holloway** Computer Artist: **Christo Holloway** Client: **Chris Collins Studio**

Photographers 192, 193

alex bee photography . 1425 rock quarry road suite 115 . raleigh nc 27610

alex bee photography . 1425 rock quarry road suite 115 . raleigh nc 27610 . 919 821 1661 f/821 4115

LAURA J. MOWERS
laura@mowersphotography.com

MOWERS PHOTOGRAPHY

1308 FOURTH STREET SOUTHEAST | MINNEAPOLIS | MN 55414

PHONE | 612.331.8211   FAX | 612.331.7522   WWW | mowersphotography.com

MOWERS PHOTOGRAPHY

1308 FOURTH STREET SOUTHEAST | MINNEAPOLIS | MN 55414

MOWERS PHOTOGRAPHY

| PEOPLE | LARGE SET | LOCATION | TABLE-TOP | FOOD |

lanny nagler
photography
56 arbor street
hartford, ct 06106
t) 860.233.4040
f) 860.236.2676

lanny nagler photography   56 arbor street, hartford, ct 06106   t) 860.233.4040   f) 860.236.2676

Design Firm: **Ritz Henton Design Group** Client: **Lanny Nagler Photography**

R.SEAGRAVES

364 Devon Drive San Rafael California 94903
phone 415.499.8680 *web* www.rseagraves.com
fax 415.499.8672 *email* shooter@rseagraves.com

R.SEAGRAVES

364 Devon Drive San Rafael California 94903
phone 415.499.8680 *web* www.rseagraves.com
fax 415.499.8672 *email* shooter@rseagraves.com

R.SEAGRAVES

364 Devon Drive San Rafael California 94903
phone 415.499.8680 *web* www.rseagraves.com
fax 415.499.8672 *email* shooter@rseagraves.com

(this spread) Design Firm: **Elixir Design Inc.** Creative Director: **Jennifer Jerde** Designer: **Jennifer Tolo** Photographer: **Richard Seagraves** Client: **Richard Seagraves**

98200

Design Firm: **Axiom Creative Group** Art Director and Designer: **Brian Fink** Creative Director: **Brian Hill** Photographer: **Mike Carroll** Client: **Mike Carroll Photography**

Photographers 200, 201

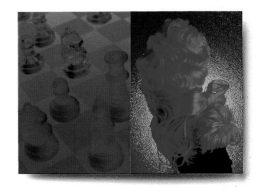

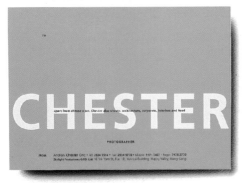

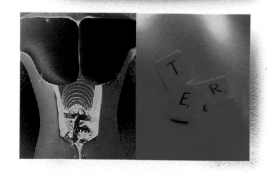

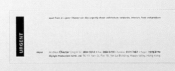

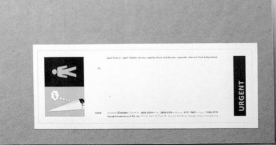

Design Firm: **Sullivan Perkins** Art Director and Designer: **Kevin Bailey** Client: **Patterson & Company**

Design Firm: **Deep Design** Art Director and Designer: **Rick Grimsley** Client: **Litho Krome Company**

Dr. Michael Smith's CELEBRATED Veterinary Collectibles Roundtable

7431 Covington Highway *Lithonia, Ga.* 30058
Telephone 770 ~ 482 ~ 5100 • Facsimile 770 ~ 484 ~ 1304

Dr. Michael Smith's CELEBRATED Veterinary Collectibles Roundtable

7431 Covington Highway *Lithonia, Ga.* 30058

Dr. Michael Smith's CELEBRATED Veterinary Collectibles Roundtable

7431 Covington Highway *Lithonia, Ga.* 30058
Telephone 770 ~ 482 ~ 5100 • Facsimile 770 ~ 484 ~ 1304

Design Firm: **Deep Design** Creative Director and Designer: **Philip Shore** Art Director: **Edward Jett** Client: **Dr. Smith's Veterinary Collectibles**

Printers, Professional Services 208, 209

FROM

READABLE *Slant* NEWSPAPER

WE ARE NOT AN ALTERNATIVE PUBLICATION

1809 WALNUT ST • PHILADELPHIA, PA • 19103

PLEASE READ ALL INFORMATION CAREFULLY

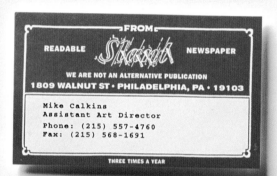

FROM

READABLE *Slant* NEWSPAPER

WE ARE NOT AN ALTERNATIVE PUBLICATION

1809 WALNUT ST • PHILADELPHIA, PA • 19103

```
Mike Calkins
Assistant Art Director
Phone: (215) 557-4760
Fax:   (215) 568-1691
```

THREE TIMES A YEAR

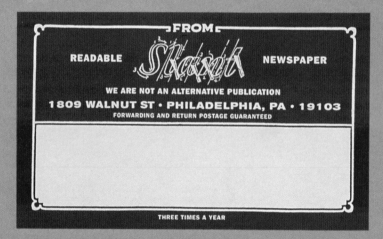

FROM

READABLE *Slant* NEWSPAPER

WE ARE NOT AN ALTERNATIVE PUBLICATION

1809 WALNUT ST • PHILADELPHIA, PA • 19103

FORWARDING AND RETURN POSTAGE GUARANTEED

THREE TIMES A YEAR

THREE TIMES A YEAR

Design Firm: **Pivot Design Inc.** Creative Director: **Brock Haldeman** Client: **Uppercase Books**

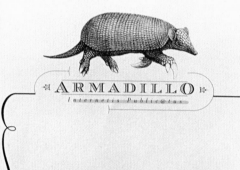

✳ ARMADILLO ✳
Internetis Public@tus

WITH COMPLIMENTS

Armadillo Internet Publishing cc
Reg No CK96/23651/23

The Manor House
14 Nuttall Gardens Morningside
Durban 4001 South Africa
P O Box 2424 Durban 4000 South Africa
Telephone +27-31-3034252
Fax +27-31-3034254
e-mail info@armadillo.co.za

http://armadillo.co.za

Armadillo Internet Publishing cc
The Manor House
14 Nuttall Gardens Morningside
Durban 4001
South Africa

P O Box 2424 Durban 4000
South Africa
Telephone +27-31-3034252
Fax +27-31-3034254
e-mail info@armadillo.co.za

http://armadillo.co.za

✳ ARMADILLO ✳
Internetis Public@tus

David Burstein

Armadillo Internet Publishing
The Manor House
14 Nuttall Gardens Morningside
Durban 4001 South Africa
P O Box 2424 Durban 4000 South Africa
Telephone +27-31-3034252
Cell 082 456 9974
Fax +27-31-3034254
e-mail dbb@armadillo.co.za

http://armadillo.co.za

Reg No CK96/23651/23 • Members **D B Burstein** BSc Hon Elec Eng (Bath UK) MSc Eng (Natal) **J C Charter** BA (Stellenbosch) **D M Forrest** BSc Eng (Natal) MSAIEE MIEE MIEEE **P C Matthews**

888 SW Fifth Avenue Suite 790
Portland OR 97204

RADIO FREE OREGON
860
AM

ALAN LAWSON
Operations Manager
alawson@kpam.com
503.552.3311

ADDRESS
888 SW Fifth Avenue Suite 790
Portland OR 97204

TEL
503.223.4321

FAX
503.294.0074

WEBSITE
www.radiofreeoregon.com

RADIO FREE OREGON
860
AM

888 SW Fifth Avenue Suite 790

Portland OR 97204   t 503.223.4321

email@kpam.com   f 503.294.0074

www.radiofreeoregon.com

RADIO FREE OREGON
860
AM

Design Firm: **Sandstrom Design** Art and Creative Director: **Steve Sandstrom** Designer: **Sarah Cook** Illustrator: **Carol Johnson** Copywriter: **Steve Sandoz** Client: **KPAM-AM 860 Radio**

KENMARK
Real Estate Group, Inc.

KENMARK
One Market, Spear Tower, 18th Floor
San Francisco, California 94105

KENMARK
Construction, Inc.

Joe Donati
Vice President
415. 908. 1544

One Market, Spear Tower, 18th Floor
San Francisco, California 94105

phone 415. 908. 2900
fax 415. 908. 2903
e-mail jdonati@kenmarkgroup.com

One Market, Spear Tower, 18th Floor
San Francisco, California 94105

phone 415. 908. 2900
fax 415. 908. 2903

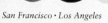

San Francisco · Los Angeles

sundance

sundance
The Sundance Group 3865 West 2400 South Salt Lake City, Utah 84120

sundance

sundance

The Sundance Group

MIKE L. WASHBURN Chief Financial Officer
3865 West 2400 South Salt Lake City, Utah 84120
Phone 801.973.4801 Fax 801.972.0874
email mike.washburn@sundance.net

MIKE L. WASHBURN | CHIEF FINANCIAL OFFICER
Group 3865 West 2400 South Salt Lake City, Utah 84120 Phone 801.973.4801 Fax 801.972.0874

ROBERT REDFORD

MÜNSTER

Road-Stop-Münster, Schiffahrter Damm 315, D-48157 Münster

Turn-Around Gaststättenbetrieb GmbH, Geschäftsführer: Thomas Decker
Road-Stop-Münster unter Lizenz der Road-Stop Franchise GmbH & Co. KG

Road-Stop-Münster, Schiffahrter Damm 315, D-48157 Münster
Tel: +49-251-32 70 170, Fax: +49-251-32 70 172, Mobil: +49-171-41 41 484, E-Mail: td@turn.around.de, Homepage: http://www.road-stop.de
Bankverbindung: Deutsche Bank Münster, KTO-Nr.: 03 333 02, BLZ: 400 700 80

ONE FREE BEVERAGE

Good For:

If you can drink it, it's on us.
Take your pick from any beverage
on the **AUTOBISTRO** *menu.*

13035

Bistro Beverages

All coffee drinks are available regular or decaffeinated. All hot beverages are 12 or 20 ounces,
and all cold beverages are 16 or 24 ounces unless otherwise noted. For an extra shot of espresso, add 50¢.

4100 Birch St (suite 108) Newport Beach CA 92660
AUTOBISTRO

.......$1.25

.......$1.25

$2.00...$3.00

.......$2.75

uice. Ask
ay.

.......$2.00

r no-wait

SPARKLING WATER.............................

SOFT DRINKS (24 oz).............................
Coke, Diet Coke, Sprite, Barq's Root Bee

WHY THERE ARE NO SUBSTITUTIONS AT AUTOBISTRO. AND WHY THERE IS NO SUBSTITU
highest restaurant quality possible, while still delivering your order quickly enough to
parking lot, we are unable to make any substitutions or changes to our menu items. Adm
less choice than at a traditional bistro, but we think you'll find the quality of the choices

FOOD

Design Firm: **Sandstrom Design** Art Director, Creative Director and Designer: **Steve Sandoz** Photographer: **Paul Foster** Copywriter: **Steve Sandstrom** Client: **Autobistro**

川

川

Design Firm: **Packaging Create Inc.** Art Director: **Akio Okumura** Designer: **Sae Nagaoka** Client: **Kawazoe**

川

大阪市北区曽根崎新地1丁目9・6
菱富ビル1階　〒530・0002
TEL 06・6456・4300
FAX 06・6456・4322

川添

川添

Caffé e Cucina presents a
passionate tradition of epic
dimensions.
LA PANARDA 'La Panarda'
celebrates memorable events
with specialty dishes from
the land and sea.

Caffé e Cucina presents a
passionate tradition of epic
dimensions.
LA PANARDA 'La Panarda'
celebrates memorable events
with specialty dishes from
the land and sea.

CAFFÉ E CUCINA
CATERING
FIRST FLOOR
FIVE FIVE THREE
CHAPEL STREET
SOUTH YARRA 3141
PHONE 03) 9827 7939
FACSIMILE 03) 9826 8355

e x p l (r u s

CANADA 36 Toronto St., Suite 1200,
Toronto, Ontario M5C 2C5
Tel: (416) 863-6400 Fax: (416) 863-6552

USA 121 E. 24th Street 11th Floor
New York, NY 10010-2912
Tel: (212) 477-7373 Fax: (212) 505-9830

e x p l O r u s

Jean Third
President

CANADA 36 Toronto Street, Suite 1200,
Toronto, Ontario, Canada M5C 2C5
Tel: (416) 863-6400 #351 Fax: (416) 863-0660
e-mail: jthird@attglobal.net

USA 121 E. 24th Street, 11th Floor
New York, NY 10010-2912
Tel: (212) 477-7373 Fax: (212) 505-9830

explorus.com

e x p l O r u s

e x p l O r u s

CANADA   36 Toronto St., Suite 1200, Toronto, Ontario M5C 2C5
USA   121 E. 24th Floor, New York, NY 10010-2912

Design Firm: Engage Advertising Art Director and Photographer: Tomasz Borowicz Creative Director: Romon Milo Client: HDS Restaurant Retail 220 221

SAN CARLO

Design Firm: **Cucco S.r.l.** Art Director: **Susanna Cucco** Designer: **Elisabetta Marzio** Client: **San Carlo**

P.ZZA SAN CARLO 195/201 10123 TO ITALIA T+39 011 5627283 F+39 011 5624891
P.ZZA SAN CARLO 169/173 10123 TO ITALIA T+39 011 5621266 F+39 011 5624891
VIA ROMA 53 10123 TORINO ITALIA T+39 011 5114111 F+39 011 5114190
S. AMM: VIA CESARE BATTISTI 2 10123 TO ITALIA T+39 011 5114111 F+39 011 5114190

SAN CARLO

SAN CARLO

700 Airport Blvd., Suite Number 200
Burlingame, California 94010
Tel [650] 579-0600   Fax [650] 579-1733
www.gymboree.com

The Gymboree Corporation
700 Airport Blvd., Suite 200
Burlingame, CA 94010-1912
Tel [650] 373-7144
Fax [650] 696-7581
gary_white@gymmail.com
www.gymboree.com

Gary White
Vice-Chairman of the Board
and Chief Executive Officer

GYMBOREE

700 Airport Blvd.

Suite Number 200

Burlingame

California 94010

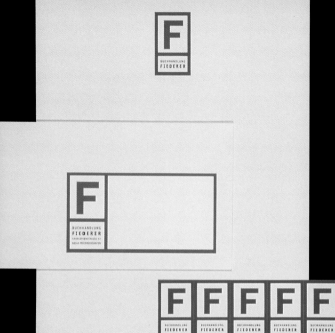

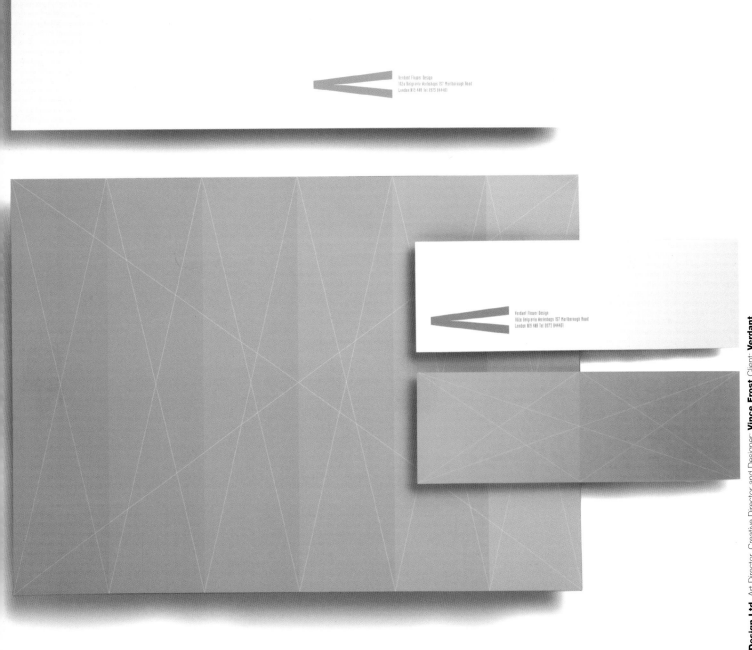

Design Firm: **Frost Design Ltd.** Art Director, Creative Director and Designer: **Vince Frost** Client: **Verdant**

LINCOLN SPORTS COMMISSION

1135 M STREET
SUITE 200
P.O. BOX 83737
LINCOLN, NE 68501

name | **Teresa Priefert**

address   1135 M STREET
            SUITE 200
            P.O. BOX 83737
            LINCOLN, NE 68501

e-mail   teresa@lincoln.org

phone   402 | 434•5343

phax   402 | 436•2360

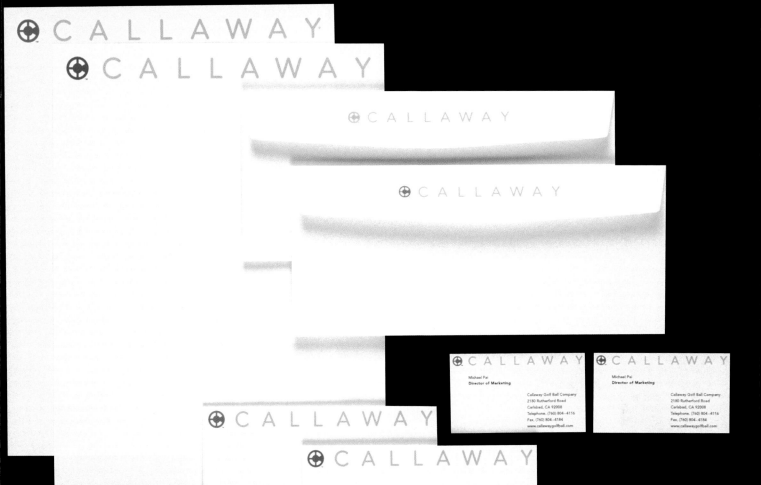

Design Firm: **Pentagram Design** Art and Creative Director: **Kit Hinrichs** Client: **Callaway**

SanomaWSOY Group

tel. +358 (0)10 51 999, fax +358 (0)10 519 5310, Martinkyläntie 11 A, 01770 Vantaa, Finland, kaupparek. nro/trade reg. no 781 529, kotipaikka/registered office Vantaa, ly-tunnus/business code fi-1592801-2

tel. +358 (0)10 51 999, fax +358 (0)10 519 5310, Martinkyläntie 11 A, 01770 Vantaa, Finland, kaupparek. nro/trade reg. no 781 529, kotipaikka/registered office Vantaa, ly-tunnus/business code fi-1592801-2

SanomaWSOY Group

ULLA JOUTSENVIRTA partnership

2ndhead
SanomaWSOY Group

mobile +358 (0)40 748 3446, ulla.joutsenvirta@2ndhead.com
2ndhead.com, fax +358 (0)10 519 5310, Martinkyläntie 11 A, FIN-01770 Vantaa

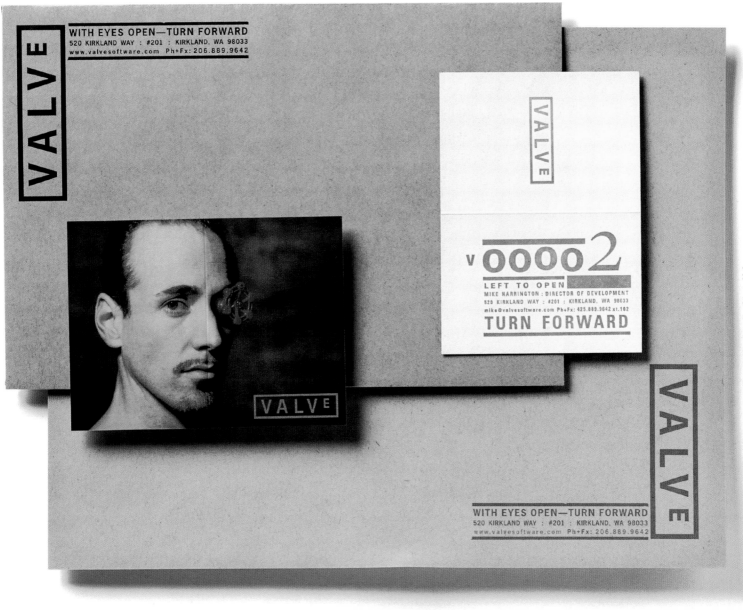

Design Firm: **The Leonhardt Group** Art Director, Creative Director, Designer and Copywriter: **Ray Ueno** Photographrapher: **Karen Moskowitz** Client: **Valve**

CORDER associates, inc.

2602 West Baseline Road Suite 22, Mesa, Arizona 85202

p 480 752 8533   F 480 752 8534

www.cordernet.com

SCOTT HARMAN

CORDER associates, inc.

2602 West Baseline Road Suite 22, Mesa, Arizona 85202

p 480 752 8533   F 480 752 8534

e sales@cordernet.com

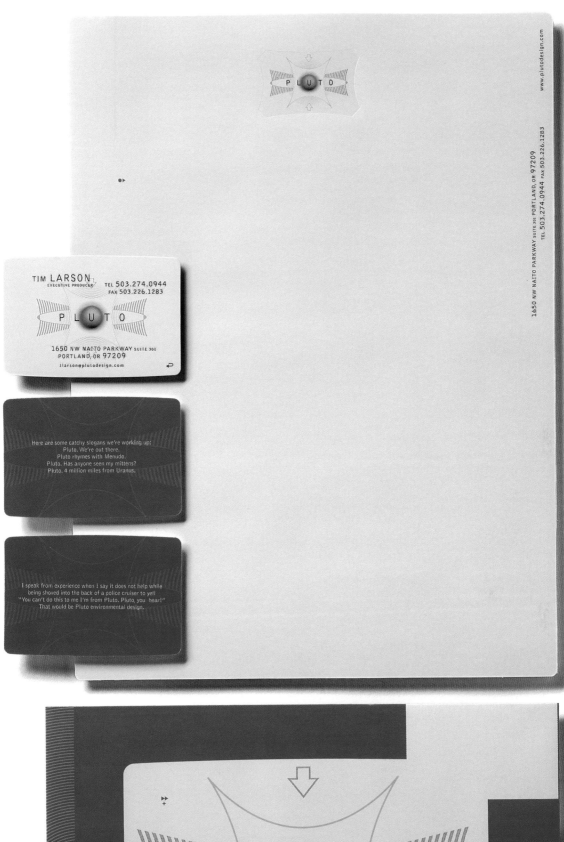

TIM **LARSON**
EXECUTIVE PRODUCER   TEL 503.274.0944
                     FAX 503.226.1283

P L U T O

1650 NW NAITO PARKWAY SUITE 301
PORTLAND, OR 97209
tlarson@plutodesign.com

Here are some catchy slogans we're working up:
Pluto. We're out there.
Pluto rhymes with Menudo.
Pluto. Has anyone seen my mittens?
Pluto. 4 million miles from Uranus.

I speak from experience when I say it does not help while
being shoved into the back of a police cruiser to yell
"You can't do this to me I'm from Pluto. Pluto, you hear!"
That would be Pluto environmental design.

1650 NW NAITO PARKWAY SUITE 301 PORTLAND, OR 97209
TEL 503.274.0944 FAX 503.226.1283

www.plutodesign.com

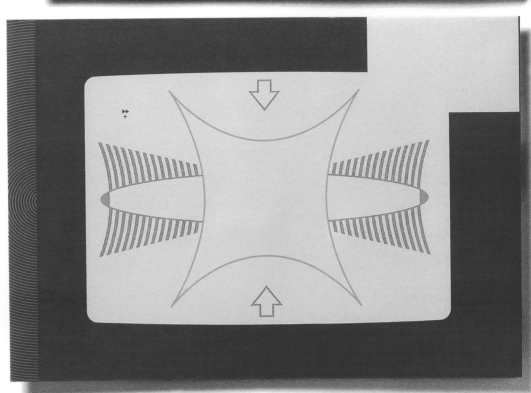

Design Firm: **Sandstrom Design** Art Director: **Jon Olsen** Creative Director: **Steve Sandstrom** Designer: **Andrew Randall** Client: **Pluto**

texas world television

twtv

Joe Cantu

texas world television

2009 108th Street Suite 905
Grand Prairie, Texas 75050
tel 214.606.1616
tel 800.551.2382
fax 214.606.2820

texas world television

2009 108th Street Suite 905
Grand Prairie, Texas 75050

2009 108th Street Suite 905
Grand Prairie, Texas 75050
tel 214.606.1616
tel 800.551.2382
fax 214.606.2820

Design Firm: **Blok Design** Art Director, Creative Director and Designer: **Vanessa Eckstein** Client: **Cisneros Television Group**

Television 234,235

MUNICIPAL | PARKING | SOLUTIONS

MUNICIPAL | PARKING | SOLUTIONS

1201 Walnut 13th Floor PO Box 410233 Kansas City MO 64141

MUNICIPAL | PARKING | SOLUTIONS

Colin M. Dobell   (816) 654-1850
President and CEO   (816) 556-2802 fax

1201 Walnut 13th Floor
PO Box 410233
Kansas City MO 64141

1201 Walnut 13th Floor PO Box 410233 Kansas City MO 64141 (816) 654-1850 Fax (816) 556-2802

Design Firm: **Brad Terres Design** Designer: **Brad Terres** Photographer: **Alan Blaustein**

THE VINEYARD INN AT CRANE RIDGE

THE VINEYARD INN AT CRANE RIDGE

5405 GREENVILLE ROAD

LIVERMORE

CA 94550

THE VINEYARD INN AT CRANE RIDGE

5405 GREENVILLE ROAD, LIVERMORE, CA 94550, TEL (925) 455-8085, FAX (925) 455-8089

Design Firm: **Chapman & Jones** Art Director and Illustrator: **Shirley Chapman** Designers: **Shirley Chapman** and **Ed Johnson** Client: **The Vineyard Inn at Crane Ridge**   Trade, Travel 238,239

LA LUNA OIL COMPANY

CARRERA 9A NO.99-02 OF.815 SANTAFÉ DE BOGOTÁ DC COLOMBIA

LA LUNA OIL COMP

LA LUNA OIL COMPANY

IVÁN FAJARDO MACHADO

President

CARRERA 9A NO.99-02 OF.815
SANTAFÉ DE BOGOTÁ DC COLOMBIA

Telephone 571 611 5626   571 257 4747

Facsimile 571 611 5766

E-mail ifajardo@impsat.net.co

TYLER CARTIER   1200 POST ALLEY / SEATTLE, WA 98101   T 206.467.1174   F 206.343.0705   E TYLER@STRIKEPLATE.COM

WWW.STRIKEPLATE.COM   1200 POST ALLEY / SEATTLE, WA 98101

WORDS WITH CREATIVE SPARK

WORDS WITH CREATIVE SPARK

WWW.STRIKEPLATE.COM

Design Firm: **Dietz Design Co.** Art Director: **Robert Dietz** Designers: **Renee Yancey** and **Robert Dietz** Client: **Strikeplate**

BOBMURPHYWRITER

150 Chestnut Street, Suite 700, Providence, Rhode Island 02903

phone: (401) 272-4613   email: murphycopy@aol.com

BOBMURPHYWRITER

NEAL G. HICKS
Executive Director
nealghicks@aol.com

**TUCSON
ZOOLOGICAL
SOCIETY**
900 S. Randolph Way
Tucson, AZ 85716
P 520/881.4735
P 520/881.1078
F 520/881.1450

**TUCSON
ZOOLOGICAL
SOCIETY**
900 South Randolph Way
Tucson, AZ 85716

TUCSON ZOOLOGICAL SOCIETY

900 S. Randolph Way	EXECUTIVE	Vice President	Past President	Oscar Campas	Deeus Martin	REID PARK ZOO
Tucson, AZ 85716	DIRECTOR	Kevin Fizsimmons	John Carlson	Sharyn Chesser	Oscar Parades, Jr.	
	Neal G. Hicks			Frank Harris	Jim Parsons	Administrator
P 520/881.4735		Secretary	DIRECTORS	Suellyn Hull	Sam Robinson	Susan Basford
P 520/881.1078		Natali Little	Barbara Abrams	Lin Hulse	Trisa Schorr	
F 520/881.1450	2000 OFFICERS		Fran Armstrong	Barbara James	Fred Shaffer	General Curator
	President	Treasurer	Gretchen Aronoff	Randi Kistel	Jane Slosser	Michael Flint
	Jocelyn Eliis	Wendy Lee	Barbara Baume	Bruce MacDonald	Ellie Werner	Education Curator
						Vivian VanPeenen

DesignersCreativeDirectorsArtDirectors

Copywriters

Photographers Illustrators

Design Firms

Clients

Subscribe to Graphis Magazine The International Journal of Design & Visual Communication In US: toll-free 1-866-648-2915 International: +1-973-627-5162 or order at www.graphis.com

Advertising Annual 2001

Annual Reports7

Poster Annual 2000

Book Design 2

Design Annual 2001

New Talent Design Annual 2000

"Caution: don't read this book unless you want to change your life. On the other hand, if you have work published here... pack your bags; you're already on your way."

Interactive Design 1

Corporate Identity 3

Packaging Design8

At fine booksellers everywhere
or order at www.graphis.com

Order Graphis on the Web from anywhere in the world: www.graphis.com